JUST TRY IT ON!

"Susan Redstone is the Christiane Amanpour of shopping. She should be given a Nobel prize."
—Simon Doonan, author, *Wacky Chicks*

"*The* must-have fashion accessory this season."
—Karen W. Bressler, co-author, *A Century of Lingerie*

"A fantastic resource fashion guide!"
—Lucy Sykes Rellie, designer and editor

"A titillating, tempting, and terrific tour of the ins and outs of fashion style."
—Phillip Bloch, celebrity stylist

JUST TRY IT ON!

A
Month by Month
Guide to
Shopping and Style

SUSAN REDSTONE

* * *

CITADEL PRESS
KENSINGTON PUBLISHING CORP.
WWW.KENSINGTONBOOKS.COM

CITADEL PRESS BOOKS are published by

Kensington Publishing Corp.
850 Third Avenue
New York, NY 10022

All Kensington titles, imprints, and distributed lines are available at special
quantity discounts for bulk purchases for sales promotions, premiums,
fund-raising, educational, or institutional use. Special book excerpts or
customized printings can also be created to fit specific needs. For details,
write or phone the office of the Kensington special sales manager:
Kensington Publishing Corp., 850 Third Avenue, New York, NY 10022,
attn: Special Sales Department; phone 1-800-221-2647.

CITADEL PRESS and the Citadel logo are Reg. U.S. Pat. & TM Off.

Illustrations by Cynthia Steffe

First printing: January 2008

10 9 8 7 6 5 4 3 2

Printed in the United States of America

Library of Congress Control Number: 2007937042

ISBN-13: 978-0-8065-2841-0
ISBN-10: 0-8065-2841-9

For Seymour and Valerie

CONTENTS

* * *

INTRODUCTION

* * *

Okay, so I've been there. And when I say I've been there, I *really* mean it. I have worn the absolute wrong thing at the absolute wrong time. I've felt embarrasseed and underdressed at a holiday party in winter, and I've chosen the wrong bathing suit and sunglasses in the summer. I'll also fess up that more than one piece of extortionately priced clothing has hung in my closert unworn, just to remind me of my mistake.

You might say that I *was* the fashion uninitiated, except that I considered myself a dedicated follower of fashion! The truth is, we all screw up sometimes. The reason for this is simple: you can have fashion *smarts* without fashion *sense*. And that is why I wrote this book. You may know what you like and buy it by the truckload, but it may not work for you personally as well as it could. And you may not be making the best wardrobe selections because you are searching for them at the wrong time. Timing is everything in fashion, as you will see as you read on. Also, having all the cool stuff and knowing when to take it out and flaunt it is a special art form. So is knowing how to plan your wardrobe options so that you do more saving than spending in the long run.

Then why would you sit up and pay attention to my scribblings? What do I know that's different from the rest? Well, I wasn't always a fashion journalist attending fashion shows, churning out articles on what's hot and new. There was a time when I, too, had no experience with fashion at all except for an undirected wanderlust for acquiring items fueled by the fantasy of flicking through the slick and enviable glossy magazine editorials. Then I began writing for the glossy magazines, which gave me access to a whole new world. Before I knew it, I was backstage at fashion shows, seeing behind the scenes, meeting photographers, interviewing designers, going on shoots, selecting clothes for TV segments, working with stylists and *watching* these professionals at work. Through all of this, I *finally* learned step by step how to navigate all the fashion faux pas. Those experiences have taught me how to translate the fashion babble and to give you the straight talk about what fashion insiders really do themselves, behind the scenes, and how your favorite stores sell must-have merchandise each year.

To bring the true fashion insider's view to a down-to-earth level, I had to ask a lot of questions and try things out for myself. In fact, that's how I coined my favorite fashion phrase, "Just Try It On!" Sometimes with fashion, you can't tell until you *just try it on.* Sure, you can scour the Internet for a coveted item and guess at your size when you spy a fabulous vintage dress at the local flea market, but you'll never know if it's truly right for you until you try it on for yourself. That's a fact.

The next piece of my fashion philosophy fell into place when I was styling fashion segments for morning TV shows like *Good Day New York* and *The CW11 Morning News.* On live TV it only made sense to borrow fashion items that were available in the stores immediately so that when I was showing and discussing how to wear things, my TV appearances would have immediate instant gratitification value to the viewers. Of course, like all journalists in news who want to be the first to break a story, it made sense for me to show off how to use the brand new merchandise of the season as soon as it hit the stores. Hence, my system and plan for month-by-month shopping was hatched. And the best part is, it's budget friendly. Choose from the largest, freshest selection of stuff, and happy with your choices made early, you can plan other areas of your wardrobe within the same season to coordinate perfectly without breaking the bank. Once you've bought great boots, your skirt choices will follow accordingly. Once you've decided on a theme or two for your summer collection, you can discipline yourself to just a few items within that range. It's all about making sure your choices are made early, as the merchandise seasonally hits the stores.

What I have learned, too, about planning TV segments for future broadcasts is the value of knowing the seasonal shipment dates. The retail end of the fashion business is on a very clear and planned schedule. If you've ever drifted round the local mall and vaguely wondered why bathing suits are in the stores when it's minus two degrees outside, this part of my plan will help make sense of all that. There's a method to the madness and it makes sense. But most of all, knowing *when* to go looking for what you want is such valuable time-saving knowledge. Even better, if you've ever had that rare shopping conundrum where you see nothing you like but you know you need *something,* it pays to know when the stores will next receive new shipments. You'll earn yourself a second chance at being the first to purchase new stuff with the best of available choices.

I hope you enjoy my unique month-to-month guide. It's packed full of tips, plans, and shopping preparations matched to making every month of the year and every moment of wardrobe filling more fun. Getting a little extra fashion savvy is little more than some clever planning, easy rules, and ways to learn to trust your instincts. You're just getting a little extra push from *Just Try It On!*

So, my hope is that as you glide through the year, ticking off the seasonal pitfalls, you will find profound success learning how to dress and shop better. No more dilemmas. My goal is to make sure that I pass on all the insider information of the fashion biz and the retail stores. In addition to the inside scoop you get from each chapter, you will also get information from the sections at the end of each month called "What to Shop in January" (month changes with each chapter) to satisfy your craving for instant gratification and "Tips for a Lower Tab" that will save you from wearing out your credit cards. Right here, right now, we can pledge together that you will never again wear or own a fashion faux pas—not even one item. My aim is to give you a happening head start, and when you are done, you will be armed with the fashion savvy to help you spend, shop, and coordinate your outfits perfectly. *Just Try It On!* will boost your fashion confidence right up there with your fabulous hair and wonderful life—which is where it should be. No matter what the occasion, from now on you will enjoy the process of confident shopping and self-styling at home *and* be your best dressed ever!

Enjoy!

Susan
xoxoxo

ACKNOWLEDGMENTS

* * *

Just Try It On! would not have taken the shape it did without the help of some very gracious fashion insiders who took the time to help round up my research. Heartfelt thanks to Boogie Weinglass, Brad Johns, designers Marc Bouwer, Jeff Mahshie, Catherine Malandrino, Nicole Miller, Betsey Johnson, Luca Orlandi, Traver Rains, and Cynthia Steffe. Also, many thanks to Jo Jeffery at Figleaves.com, Ann Watson at Henri Bendel, and teams of people at Aerosoles, Liz Claiborne, Safilo USA, H&M, La Force & Stevens, Lady Foot Locker, Steve & Barry's, JCPenney, and the various marketing departments of countless more brands of apparel I have styled with over recent years. You know who you are!

Sincere thanks to my publisher at Kensington Publishing; to Danielle Chiotti, a brilliant and endlessly enthusiastic editor; and to my literary agent Elisabeth Weed at Trident Media who took on this project without a moment's hesitation. Extra special thanks to the tireless, good-humored dedication and legal advisements of attorney Michael "Superman" Marcus.

I could not have written *Just Try It On!* without the influence and support of other exceptional writers who served as inspiration and resources. They also happen to be dear friends. Thanks to Richard Torregrossa who pushed me to put pen to paper in the first place and to Syl Tang who kept me at the sharp edge of hip and cool and offered unique and relevant insights. Heaps of gratitude to Laurie Schechter for her knowledge, experience, and resourcefulness that knows no bounds and for her generosity in sharing it. And to Karen Brooks with whom I co-authored previous books, I owe a debt of thanks for opening up this end of the writer's market.

And finally, an acknowledgment of familial influences. Grandma Annie was a dedicated seamstress who spent hours altering so much of my childhood and teen wardrobe. Memories of her will never fade. Nor will those of cousin Lilian Fenster, a Brit-turned-true-Park-Avenue style icon and world-class shopper. She introduced me to American fashion yet constantly reminded me to appreciate European tailoring. Big thanks to her daughter Barbara Smithen who gave me my first Hermès scarf and continues to share everything she knows about costume jewelry including loaning me her most outrageous and valuable pieces. Deepest thanks to my dad and brother Danny for being the most rewarding pair to buy gifts for, I have imposed fashion taste on both for decades, and they show their appreciation by literally wearing their duds to threads. Ditto for Shorty the cat who never objects to a fashionable collar change and who has always been present for every word I have written. Last but not least, love and thanks to Mum who is my favorite partner in shopping crime and whose *less-is-more* style has been a leveling influence throughout my life. If, when we shop together, I *just try something on* and she looks over and says, *"Just take it off,"* she is usually right.

JUST TRY IT ON!

Your Fashion Emergency Kit (F.E.K.)

*I*t's a New Year, a new you, and this year you're going to be your best fashion incarnation ever. You probably already know what's in, what's out, and what's heinous on you. So why not start the year with a little preparation that is as much a personal positive-reinforcing ritual as a style lifesaver? That's where your Fashion Emergency Kit (F.E.K.) comes in. Getting ready for a new year equipped with such a kit should ward off fashion disasters from the very start. It's also fun to have a project at the beginning of the New Year to keep you motivated. And motivation is exactly what you'll be getting if you start right now by putting together your F.E.K.

WHY HAVE A KIT?

It all starts with a bag of stuff. But not just any kind of stuff. The F.E.K. should be a staple of your life. It is your security blanket during a work wardrobe malfunction and a friend in need at your best friend's wedding. It helps you attain a level of confidence and preparedness that makes you feel protected. It is like fashion insurance! No matter whether you spend all your time in the office or in the car or on the freeway or on the plane or at your boyfriend's house, your kit will be for those foul fashion moments and save the day.

The greatest thing about the F.E.K. is that you prepare it while you're at the top of your game and feeling your best—and it comes to your rescue when you're feeling your very worst. Of course, life's little fashion mishaps don't just happen in one given environment (although for some reason the office is a notorious offender in the fashion disaster department), and so in achieving your Zen-like state of perpetual preparedness and fashion perfection, you should have multiple kits. Because with your F.E.K. stashed away in a bottom desk drawer at work or in the trunk of the car or under your boyfriend's bed, you have the wherewithal to make a fashion fix. Whether or not it's a ripped sleeve, unexpected doggie hair on black pants, or a garden variety mishap like snagged hosiery, don't underestimate the power of fashion preparedness. It only takes a few minutes and a few cents to make up your kit, and you may already have the key items in your home.

Only you know what personal items you may want to add. No two F.E.K.s are alike as they're created specifically for your individual needs. My personal F.E.K travels with me between cities when I'm working on the road, and it's always personalized with a spare mascara—a key beauty item for me—as well as a $20 bill, because I *always* need cash. It always contains my most trusted medicines too. I can't tell you how many times other people that I'm working with have been grateful for the Advil that's lurking in my kit! Having a higher level of preparedness doesn't just benefit you; it can help your friends or family too. Think of it as your private secret weapon that'll bail you out when fashion, beauty, or other emergencies strike!

One of the greatest things about the F.E.K. is that it's a great place to offload some of those items that you don't use all the time but can't quite toss out when you have a wardrobe purge.

How to Prep the Kit

The key to having a great F.E.K. is thoughtful preparation. So kit prepping is simply figuring out your exact personal requirements. Try to set aside an hour one evening and get prepping!

1. **Get an old tote, a large makeup case, or any bag that you don't use much anymore.** In a pinch, use a large transparent ziplock baggie. It's not glamorous, but it's oh-so-useful as you can easily see everything inside at a glance. There is one veteran New York stylist who wouldn't *think* to use anything but an extra large ziplock plastic baggie, because of the ease of visibility and access.

2. **Make a list of the items you think you'll need most in your bag.** If you're feeling stuck for ideas, check your list against the lists that follow, which is a rough guide to the sorts of things professional stylists swear by in their kits.

3. **Fill the bag, following your list, with a selection of basics that fits your fashion life.** This little exercise will force

you to think about what you need, what you don't need, and what you might have never thought you needed but could really use.

F.E.K. essentials

F.E.K. essentials should each carry its own weight because they all comprise the backbone of your kit. Some things listed will be more naturally useful to some than others. For example, if you have a dog, perhaps your double-sided tape for pet hair pick-up should be super-sized!

* *Double-sided tape:* Great for taping up hems on pants and skirts—that is until you get them to the tailor or get them home to repair yourself. It is pretty cool to be instantly able to tape up your dropped hem. Double-sided tape is also great for picking up unintended doggie or kitty hair from pants, sweaters, or other apparel, so you can skip the lint remover roller and save room in your F.E.K. Say no more: just say yes to double-sided tape.

* *Needle and thread:* This may seem obvious to some but not to all, so put them in. It's also smart to add spare buttons—one white and one black. Small is best. If you've been lucky enough to stay in a hotel where the sewing kit was complimentary, then toss it into your kit—now that's a fine, fine shortcut. (Note to self: take the sewing kit next time you're away in a hotel.) If you don't have a sewing kit, you can make one in a flash. Next time you sit down with a soda in front of your favorite sitcom, prepare some sewing needles. Thread a few needles with white, taupe, and black thread. Next, find a matchbook and remove the actual matches. Then, sew each needle halfway through the

cardboard from the inside to the outside and back down to the inside. This will ensure that the sharp ends are away from fingers, and you can close the cover for safe storage.

✱ *Nonaerosol travel-size vial of hairspray:* Here's another double-duty item. Hairspray isn't just for flyaway hair actually, but for the static cling on your skirt. Spray your knees and your skirt will leave them alone. Pretty genius!

✱ *Spare hose:* Okay. So perhaps you're not a big hose fan or even a wearer. You may think, *no hose needed here*. But consider this: maybe one day, some dark, opaque hose will keep you warm if worn under your pants on a snowy, rainy, or cold day. I'll bet you have an old pair of warm hose you never use that are clogging up your sock drawer and that could be just as happily housed in your F.E.K.

✱ *Clear nail polish:* It's not just for nails! Keep this item in your F.E.K. for sticking down and patching ripped hose. At the first sign of a rip or tear in your hose, don't remove them! While still wearing them, apply clear polish to each end of the tear and sit still while it dries. When the polish dries, it creates a hard seal at the edges of the tear preventing it from spreading further. Clear polish is the most invisible and the best to use, but if the tear is in a hidden place, colored polish will do. Don't worry if the polish seeps through and sticks to the skin on your leg, it will peel off later!

✱ *Umbrella:* A portable, collapsible umbrella, for those days when you look fine, and so does your hair, and the weather does its best to change *all* that.

✱ *A white shirt:* Wrinkle free, if possible, since it may be stashed in your F.E.K. for months before you use it. It doesn't need to be fancy or from the fabulous Thomas Pink. If you've had a clumsy day and your lunch has ended up down your front, a fresh shirt that will go with everything will serve you well. If you're not a fan of white shirts, black will also work just as well.

* *Hair accessories:* Stash items that you normally wear. Please, not the floral leftovers from that wedding party or hair bands in bright velvet that are not a normal part of your fashion repertoire. Keeping sparkly barrettes, pretty jewel-encrusted bobby pins, elastic hair bands, and other decorative hardware and soft elastics for dressing up, pinning up, tying up, or restraining hair up or into a tight pony tail will help you ward off bad hair days.

* *Baby wipes:* A portable, resealable pack, please. Sounds a bit naughty, but in a pinch, these are the magic towels that remove makeup stains from sweaters, smeared eye makeup, grime from hands, dirt from under nails, and mayo from lunch that landed on your pants. They're not as good as the dry cleaners, but they come pretty close and are a great way to do a triage on your clothes! Shout stain removal wipes are very cool too, though of course these only do the job on clothing but *can't* be used on your hands or face too.

* *An extra sweater, jacket, sweatshirt, or shawl:* Sweatshirts are for the boyfriend's house kit or gym bag kit. Shawls are feminine and flexible and fold small so they're perfect for an airplane kit, office kit, or boyfriend's house kit. Knit sweaters are for the car kit or office kit, and so are jackets.

* *A comfortable pair of flats:* Not your fanciest pair, just a pair that you can walk in, and fast. A dark or neutral

color is best. They'll cover for a necessary and überquick errand dash or save your suede Jimmy Choos from the rain at lunchtime. And that pair of worn-out sneakers that have no life left in from the gym? Don't toss them—they'll do for your office kit too, especially if you live in a walk-up or work in a high-rise. Fire escapes and stairwells don't mix with Manolos. Keep those smelly old sneakers in the kit, 'cause ya *just* never know.

On-location kits

On-location kits are the perfect answer to any multitasking alpha female's life. The idea is to keep and tailor kits specifically for where you will be. So whether your jam-packed life is full of spontaneous moments or revolves around a predictable but crazy routine, creating especially customized multiple kits and storing them in different locations is great fashion insurance.

Car kit. If you're planning a kit for the car, think smart. If you spend a lot of time outdoors, perhaps a spare baseball cap is the big kit-specific hit here. Or maybe it's sunscreen or bug spray. A tightly rolled towel, windbreaker, or travel umbrella may also come in handy. You won't know how grateful you are for a spare pair of sunglasses until you misplace yours en route somewhere (gasp!) and face the prospect of driving without them. You'll be thanking me from the bottom of your kit if you pull out a spare to get you on your way.

Boyfriend kit. A kit for your boyfriend's house might include extra lingerie, perfume, a great book, or a do-it-yourself manicure set (if he's intent on watching the tube all weekend!). And don't forget all those girl-friendly bits that he's not likely to have lying around his home: tampons, panty liners, hairspray, lip balm, and slouchy socks for vegging out. Also, if your man is the spontaneous type who plans overnight trips at the last minute, perhaps consider stashing some fresh underwear, a bathing suit, a warm sweater, and a medium-weight all-season jacket too.

Gym kit. A kit for the bottom of your gym bag may contain extra makeup or hair products for when the change of plans calls for heading out on the town post-workout. Some deodorant, spare socks, spare shoe laces, an extra sports bra, or an old swimsuit, one you don't care about getting saturated with chlorine (for a change of workout—in the pool maybe?) can all make a visit to the gym run more smoothly.

F.E.K. extras

These little "extras" may be unglamorous, but be assured, they're worth taking note of. Luckily, they're all small in size and don't take up much room. Often, they're the most lifesaving items you'll have. Once your friends know you have a kit they'll ask for these, too, so it's best to stash them in multiples.

* *Tampons:* Yup, not glamorous, but without these, your fashion emergency in white jeans or pants will be a *whole* lot worse.

* *Underwear:* Panties, smalls, whatever you wish to call them—keep them in your kit. Any pair will do, but a nude thong would be the best underpinning for most outfits in a pinch.

* *Money:* Money talks, let's face it. But we're not talking about keeping a mutual fund in your kit, just a $20 bill

to save you from another trip to the ATM. A spare $20 bill has never come to any harm hidden away for an emergency. Possible uses include buying breath mints; paying taxi fare home when you've worn white or cream and the weather is inclement; taking a taxi home for a real emergency, not just a fashion one; buying a cheap new pair of gloves from a street vendor for when you lose half your pair in the cold; or purchasing a scarf when you miscalculated the weather and find yourself underdressed. You can even use it for a replacement umbrella when your F.E.K. umbrella breaks at lunchtime.

* *Stick moisturizer:* This looks like a glue stick, and it's great for hair flyaways. Just rub some on your palms and smooth down on your part. It also doubles up as a spot-target moisturizer for lips, elbows, or hands.

* *Your meds:* Pills, medicines, or tonics for whatever ails you, whether it's for a migraine moment or a really bad PMS day. Keep a pouch with your preferred headache, cramp, or indigestion meds on hand.

So there you go. You're officially equipped. It's up to you how small or large you make your kits, but the essentials for fashion-failure prevention are at your fingertips. Hopefully, you won't need one piece from it, but you've got it if you need it.

WHAT TO SHOP NOW!

So here comes the exciting part: The annual merchandising calendar is possibly one of the most overlooked aspects of shopping that, as a consumer, you can use to your advantage. Getting the insider scoop on buying, shipping dates, and merchandising habits of retail stores helps alleviate *so* much fashion stress! Armed with this information month by month, you will know when and what to look for and make smart decisions on whether it is a good idea to buy. After a while, shopping with an eye on the next season to come will become second nature, and you will automatically gravitate toward honing your style for the months ahead, picking out the best on the racks.

What hits the racks and when?

As a savvy shopper, you should know that retailers and suppliers have an actual calendar that they live by in the world of fashion. Manufacturers' shipments are not haphazard. There are actual delivery dates for when specific categories of clothing such as jeans, swimwear, and sweaters arrive in the stores each season. The following information isn't supposed to read like some "annual report" from some boring company, but if you scan on, you'll see that everything we look forward to buying is all planned out to arrive ready to hit the racks at particular times of the year.

It's genius really that stores receive the new stock for the season *way* before it's time to wear it. This gives savvy shoppers like you plenty of time to browse, buy, and store away cool finds to be worn later in the year. The idea is to keep an eye on the upcoming season on the calendar, as the fashion cycle is constantly moving forward. Seeing new clothes in the stores that can be worn immediately (and buying them) is very gratifying, but seeing items for seasons that seem a long way off is an early warning signal that the new season is a lot closer than you may think! These new wares must be shopped before the best picks are gone! The pattern that manufacturers use remains practically the same year in, year out, so if we learn from it, it'll always be helpful. For example, if you're searching for denim, the best picks hit stores in August and September. But what if you miss the window or can't find anything that you really love? No worries! Another shipment of new denim hits in February and March, too, so that you have two great opportunities to go look. With this knowledge in mind, you can get what you want the moment it hits the racks.

Take a peek at the merchandizing schedule, but don't get overawed! You don't need to purchase *all* the categories during each month. It's just a roundup of what's available! You'll learn the best moment for making one or two key purchases each month as we work through the year guide.

Another thing to remember is that not all fashion delivery charts look the same. The list that follows is gleaned from a variety of boutique owners, specialty stores, department stores, and large chain retailers, and it is meant to be general. The idea is to get you *thinking* ahead about what you will need next and what items to expect when. For the *exact* dates of arrivals in your favorite shop, you are going to have to go in and ask. That is why a friendly salesperson or personal shopper with whom you keep in touch is your best ally here. But more on that later.

THE ANNUAL MERCHANDISING SCHEDULE

JANUARY

Workout clothes
Winter scarves
Gloves
Sneakers
Transitional or seasonless clothes (lightweight wool
   sweaters, cardigans, or classic white shirts)
Spring coats

FEBRUARY
Spring shoes
Lingerie
Spring cashmeres
Denims (first delivery date)
Select swimwear
Prom dresses

MARCH
Sunglasses
Denims (second delivery date)
Spring occasion dresses
Spring pocketbooks
Early swimwear or spring break swimwear

APRIL
Main summer swimwear
Pants
Summer dresses
Spring coats
Summer shoes

MAY
Shorts
Tanks and tees
Short sleeve blouses
Lightweight dresses

JUNE
Trend swimwear
Skimpy dresses
Skimpiest tanks
Lightweight fall denim
Early fall cashmeres

JULY
 Fall transition denim
 Long sleeve tees
 Lightweight wool sweaters

AUGUST
 Main fall/winter denim
 Fall suits
 "It" bags
 Classic winter coats
 Winter skirts
 Occasion dressing (formalwear)
 Back-to-school basics
 Boots
 Flats

SEPTEMBER
 Handbags
 Party dresses
 Boots
 Hats
 Fur fashions

OCTOBER
 Holiday outfits
 Evening clutches
 Long sleeved tees
 Winter denim
 Sweaters
 Warm parkas, dressy coats, and evening coats like
  those with luxury fur trim, beading, or other
  embellishments
 Jeans
 Party shoes

Early fashionable holiday gifts such as sweaters and
lots of unsized items such as wraps, scarves, hats,
cufflinks, ties, and pajamas

NOVEMBER
Faux shearling jackets
Glamorous evening tops with embellishments like
sequins
Seasonless separates or items that work for cold
weather as well as warm such as white shirts,
denim, chinos, and cotton sweaters
Lingerie and pajamas
Gifts

DECEMBER
Resort outfits
Holiday gifts
Transitional items

As if this wasn't enough information, the categories are often
broken down by deliveries called Spring, Summer, Fall 1,
Fall 2, Winter, Holiday and Resort, but again, consider and
keep in mind that each different store makes up its own
variations of this schedule. If you want to know where the
"newest" items are in your favorite boutique or store, just
remember that the newest hottest items will be displayed
on the mannequins, front and center, so you can instantly
see what's the latest as you step inside.

As you've probably already noticed, the clothing cycle is
always a few months ahead of the weather and lifestyle patterns that normally dictate when we buy clothing.

However, there are some critical points in the calendar:
February marks the time of year for the best lingerie and
underwear, perhaps because of Valentine's Day, but also it's

just the moment when all the new styles in this category arrive in the stores. February is also the first time in the year you might see a delivery of denims, but they won't be much different from a second delivery closely scheduled in March.

Bathing suits come out in full force in April—well before we need to wear them but perfect timing for all those fashion-following spring breakers. June is a bit of a transition month as stores begin to stock their racks with cooler weather pieces, pre-fall items, and outfits you can wear immediately—lighterweight summer denims and new tees. Retailers with very fast fashion schedules with shipments every few weeks may have a short burst of bathing suits and trendy summer items (possibly something a celebrity has been seen wearing and is becoming widely copied).

When August hits, most stores will be bursting at the seams with great back-to-school staples like jeans, as August marks the biggest push of the year for new denims. They will also be teeming with sweaters, skirts, boots, and coats. PS: Coats is the one category that really only hits once a year, so you really should go look at the coats in August, the moment they arrive, if you know you need new outerwear. Since there are no new shipments of coats past August, this may be your only chance to score the coat you like in a size that fits.

September is great for hot bags, evening party dresses, and winter scarves and hats. By October the holiday party dresses are out in full force as are accessories like cashmere, and that's because sweaters are the biggest holiday fashion-gift item. There will also be some chic belts and satin clutches. Chunky knits are a hit at this time of year as well. Halfway through October comes all the glitter, sequins, gold, and metallics for the holiday season. The evening coats, too, that match these may have luxury trim like beading and other embellishments. November is a great month to pick up great last minute party tops as well as other sequined items, pajamas, and holiday lingerie. The last major marker of the year is, not surprisingly, holiday gifts, which will also appear in November. December finishes off the year with resort outfits or collections of warm-weather items such as linen pants, short sleeve shirts, dresses and coordinating bathing suits, beach accessories, sarongs, and sandals, all ready to be purchased by those lucky enough to go away for some winter sun. Resort swimwear is usually a completely different selection from what becomes available in March.

So now you have an insider's view of the annual calendar. Those who work in the fashion business use this information to their benefit and now you can too. Irene Newman, women's design director at Steve & Barry's, a lifestyle-driven specialty retailer, says, "If I see something in a magazine I like, I feel I have a head start. Because I work in the business, I know exactly when that piece will arrive and can go get it, so I won't be disappointed." With your newfound knowledge, you, too, can reap the benefits of a fashion insider. Before you know it, you'll be shopping like a true member of the fashion cognoscenti!

However, the question remains, Where should you start shopping, the big stores or the boutiques? Generally, the difference between big stores and boutiques is that where large chains will roll out a new season's collections on a schedule (often in block collections with color themes), smaller boutiques will bring in a flow of merchandise in smaller quantities at more frequent intervals, sometimes with more unique pieces. Designer Tracy Reese, for example, who has her own dedicated namesake boutique, gets about ten shipments a year. And this means the very first spring shipment may actually arrive as early as January. So you can see, things vary greatly according to the size of the retail business.

Another thing about boutique shopping is that smaller stores can sometimes cancel shipments when the weather is funky. So if you see something you really love in a boutique, it's better to buy it when you see it. If it's been very cold all winter and through part of the spring, smaller stores may cancel early spring orders, as there's no time to move this stock before summer inventory arrives. Similarly, boutiques are more adaptable to changes and are ready to add additional styles when they're selling really well.

Big stores are just as useful to you, as long as you get to know their schedules too. Big stores often have more sizes and more variety, because they have more space. It's a time-saver because all your choices are collected in one area and because you can see a wide range of options quickly. In addition, if they don't have your size or color in a style you want, they can often call another of their store locations and find it for you.

The true trick to getting the insider scoop from both boutiques and big stores is to cultivate a relationship with a sales associate. Ask her to call you when new stuff arrives, that way there are no wasted shopping trips. As Ann Watson, vice president fashion director at Henri Bendel in New York, says, "The only and truly best way to be in the know about the latest deliveries is to build a relation-

Style File

If you are the type of person who prefers clothing that shows less skin, even in the warmer months of summer, pick as much of your summer wear in the spring as possible because by July the clothing in the stores becomes very skimpy because of the hot weather.

ship with a salesperson. When that relationship is in place, the salesperson will call, as our sales staff regularly do and set things aside for you before they make it to the sales floor."

Also, retailers have stores they call their A Stores and B stores, like a city flagship and a small-town outlet of the same company, which may carry all pieces produced by name designers every season. Some even have C stores and D stores, categorized this way because of the number of shoppers they receive at out-of-the-way locations and because they may only carry a few select designer items for a smaller market. It's commonsense that there will be more choices in the larger city flagships, but that's not a good reason to avoid smaller locations. Sometimes these locations have great racks of fresh pieces for you to look through. In addition, chain stores that have locations in different states can be helpful, even though you can't get to them personally.

In warmer climates, department stores may change their winter items to spring ones faster. Not all categories of clothing will appear at the same time as they do in other stores simply because the lifestyle is different. Just keep all this information in mind no matter where you live or where you travel. For example, if you spy a fab coat in a department store in New York but they don't have it in your size, that doesn't mean you have to give up. Make a few calls and see if another branch of the store carries it. Every store is different based on clientele, but most will carry a small sampling of the stock of which an item in

Style File

Boutiques or smaller stores in general won't offer resort clothes at all unless it's suitable for their specific market.

your size could be one of them! So be persistent if there is something you really, *really* want and chase it down.

Even the shoe stores keep to a cycle. Sure, there are a few retailers that have a constant flow of new product every month, but most stores adhere to a typical Spring, Summer, Transition, Fall, and Winter schedule. Stores often put out transitional shoes—shoes that work for cold weather when it is about to turn warm or vice versa. These items can often have a six-month shelf life. They meet the demand for the "shoulder seasons" or weeks when the weather is unpredictable, and no one can tell when it will turn from spring to summer or from summer to fall. Transitional products are great, as they mean you potentially have stuff to wear between the very hot and very cold months.

One more thing: even though there is a rough time line for merchandising, our consumer-driven society has made retailers add more shipments to the original schedule. Shoppers want new stuff as trends unfold. These "extra" shipments are planned, but are often smaller in size, with fewer newer trendy items. The really low priced, high-fashion stores such as the ever-popular H&M puts out new collections every six weeks following the trends from the world's runways.

The H&M new merchandise arrives daily at stores, so the stock is continually updated, even though its fashion year consists of two main seasons: Spring/Summer and Fall/Winter. Its buying, for example, varies on the climate and country and adapts to the sales data from the stores. Sometimes the time it takes for clothing to be designed, manufactured, and delivered to the stores is as short as two weeks. This is as fast as it gets in fashion. But it can also be as long as six months, which is the classic follow-up period after buyers preview collections in the fashion capitals of London, New York, Paris, and Milan. Fashion shows in September and October, for example, preview what will be available in the spring and summer of the following year. But most importantly, these shows spawn the "trends" that will filter down to lesser-priced clothes available for all. The department store JCPenney, for example, in addition to its main shipments, now gets monthly deliveries of "fast fashion"—a good example of extra shipments designed specifically to jump on and send out the latest trends.

Clothes that arrive fast in the stores for wearing right away are known as product that is bought "in season" (at the very moment when we will wear it) or "close to season" (which might mean only a few weeks away). As Ann Watson says, "Always try to get to the store early as bestsellers and key items are gone fast!" Magazines and especially Hollywood celebrities being photographed in hot items drives sales, and as a result, merchandise comes in and moves out quicker than it ever has. When it comes to the "in season" items, buy them when you see them, because the cool stuff just won't be there in a couple of weeks!

So, no matter where you shop, think the three Fs:

* Find
* Future
* Fashion

If you find something you know you will want to wear later, get it when you see it, even if it feels too early to wear it. Later you will be grateful.

WHAT TO SHOP IN JANUARY

* Sneakers
* Sweats
* Workout gear
* Cashmere sweaters
* Spring coats
* Winter scarves and gloves

January should be your month for seeking new *sneakers, sweats,* and *athletic wear.* You can't get more motivated to restart your healthy living and exercise program than getting decked out in new workout gear. Treat yourself to good-quality, new workout shoes, picking the type to suit your most regular workout. And if you're a bona fide workout buff who really gets mileage out of those running shoes, this is your annual bookmark to upgrade your shoes and get a piece of the latest technology. You can't forget how long you've had your cross-training sneakers if you replace them at the beginning of each New Year, every year.

That lovely bouncy feel of new shoes should put a spring in your step and take you a couple of steps closer to the gym. And there's nothing quite as motivating for a new workout program than a great pair of new sweats. If you've not bought new workout fabrics made from the lightest performance materials with places to store your house keys and with the grooviest light reflectors for those nighttime jogs, go look at them now. Some sweats breathe and wick sweat away from the skin; others are made from four-way stretch high-quality fabric. Yet more have cool pockets to stash your iPod. But if you're not going to splurge on the really expensive stuff, stick to 100 percent cotton items. These wash the best, breathe for comfort, and feel the best next to skin. You may be stunned by how the newest technology boosts your workout! If your gym has a store, this is a great, great place to start. Buying gym clothes while you're at the gym (if you can) is a stroke of genius. Many of the larger gyms now feature attached stores with some of the latest and greatest athletic wear items. Whether or not you purchase them just after or before you work out, you really end up feeling inspired and that you deserve them! You're already in the workout groove, and it's a boost to continue on with your exercise program.

January is an odd month for retailers after the holidays, with a mixture of leftovers and in-between season items. This can be a great time to find *cashmere sweaters* if the weather has been mild. Retailers will be dumping the sweaters at reduced prices faster than you can say credit card. It's also the month of the year that the stores seem to be in the most chaos, and you may even find sweaters on sale that the staff forgot to put out at full price earlier in the season!

The spare winter scarves and gloves usually get merchandized close to the sweaters, so take a peek at these, too, just while you're at it—there are occasionally some really good buys to be found.

Finally, if you really can't resist and you see a novelty *spring coat* that you just know you'll wear to death, go ahead because it may not stick around for long. But only if you can't live without it!

The January sales—should I or shouldn't I?

As a general rule, most department stores begin marking down merchandise in December because they know they have to move it by February. These markdowns peak in January with blowout sales.

If you are a diehard sales shopper, the next recommendation may not earn popularity points, but it needs to be said. Some people are sales shoppers, but the big perennial sales often yield more duds than good finds. Here, simply put, is the case for steering clear of the big sales. *In general* the oddball selection and variety of sizes, colors, and styles in the sales don't necessarily offer up a good enough reason to shop them. Then consider the fact that should you find something cool, like a top or even a discounted designer dress that other people, especially if the sale is in your hometown, will have already been seen wearing. Last, who has ever, in the history of the world, heard of anyone shopping a sale rack in record fast time? Fact is, it never happens! It's time-consuming stuff and no guarantee for a successful buy. Often sale items cannot be returned, and you may not make a wise decision in the mayhem that is sale shopping. Couldn't you think of a better way to spend your precious time? Consider skipping the sales rack altogether and sort out your closet at home with the time you save. So hold on tight to your pocketbook at all times when you can in January! If you feel tempted to head for a sale and you want to resist or you are at a sale and trying hard to be good, work on keeping the following concept in your head: better to pay $200 for something that is full retail and *perfect* for you that you will wear two hundred times versus something bought hastily in a sale for $100 that never gets worn once.

If you are a true sales hound and you *must* go to a sale, go during the first few days of the sale, so things are not totally picked over. Ann Watson, whose customers get regular advance mailings, says, "If you are a regular customer at a store, you might receive a postcard or a call to signal the beginning of the sale." So be sure to get on the mailing lists of your favorite stores, check the paper for ads that give sale dates and previews, and heed anything that you get in the mail from your favorite shops.

Sale Shopping Do's and Don'ts

If you must attend the sales, *please,* don't make the classic pitfall mistakes! Heed these rules:

DON'T BUY IT IF:

- It's not your size
- It's not your style
- It's not what you need
- It's a duplication of items you already have at home
- It's not "your" color
- It's trendy and going to be out soon
- It's a random (maybe even slightly damaged) piece from a top luxury designer with the price slashed in half.

DO BUY IT IF:

- You loved it when it was full price
- It's in your size
- It's in your preferred color
- It's relevant right now, and you can wear it right away (like an evening gown for a specific event)
- It's a classic item that's been on your list (cashmere sweater, Hermès scarf, ballet flats, white shirt)

TIPS FOR A LOWER TAB

Every fashion lover wants to save money. So in each chapter you'll get a suggestion on finding ways to save on the items covered in the chapter. Some of it is innovative do-it-yourself (DIY), which is often so very satisfying and the least costly option. You'll also find other shopping and spending ideas for keeping more cash in your pocketbook. You don't need to miss out on your heart's fashion desires. Just always keep in mind that when you buy early, you can save by buying less, with the goal of owning only pieces that work really hard for you. January is no exception, especially when there is very little new and inspiring merchandise in the stores after the sales. However, New Year's workout resolutions deserve and need new athletic wear. Luckily, this is one of the easiest fashion categories to do new on a dime.

If you're not much of an exercise buff and you find yourself surrounded by workout gear right after the New Year, rather than running up your credit card bill on workout clothing you won't use, go to a general discount store like Target or Wal-Mart. There you can find pants, tanks, and hoodies. Or you can go to a specialty lifestyle store with *permanent* bargain-basement prices like Steve & Barry for sweats. Since Sarah Jessica Parker's brilliant line called Bitten appeared at this user-friendly store, shoppers have discovered the amazing array of discount priced sweats countrywide. So don't hold back. Fresh sweats are just as good, and they all go down the same hole, into the washer, over and over and over. But never, *ever* skimp on the footwear! Be sure to go to a dedicated athletic store like Lady Foot Locker and get help picking out the correct sneaker for you and your proposed physical activity.

Although there *are* trendy new styles of workout clothes

and sneakers each year, all that really matters is that your workout sneakers are new, with no mileage on them, completely unworn. Your knees and back and your whole body deserves a properly constructed pair of sneakers made especially for the sport or activity you will partake in. There is nothing wrong with having a brand name sneaker from a past season; they will support your feet and knees just the same. If you can find an outlet store, last year's hot Pumas (if they are on sale) will save you. Even check out athletic apparel dedicated to past season items on sale. So in the post–New Year season, do yourself a favor and move your old sneakers to your F.E.K. immediately—your feet will thank you for it.

If you are a dedicated hardbody and work out every day, you can splurge and buy some stuff from a specialty retailer or your gym and mix it up with stuff from discount fashion retailers like T. J. Maxx, which carries all kinds of top brands on clearance department store items.

Once you have gotten your new workout clothes in order and checked out your favorite stores for sweater deals, make a conscious effort not to spend on any other fashion items during the month of January. Think of it as Financial Detox! In addition, with all the stock being so picked over, it's better to wait. Why would you buy day-old bread if you could just hold out for a little while longer and get some fresh? Before you know it, January will be on the out and you can start over.

So as the year kicks off, your fashion radar will be tuned in to the merchandising schedules of your favorite stores, giving you the best possible opportunity to act on every fashion whim. Armed with your F.E.K., which, hopefully, you have stocked with things you *already* have in your home, you'll be able to face the fashion forecast with confidence. If you stick to the guidelines of not spending heavily this month, your finances can begin to catch up. But don't fret. If you're ready to reinvent yourself with a fashion makeover but fear you'll be short of cash, you can relax. As we move on to February, the entire chapter is dedicated to the most inventive and innovative ways of getting style for less.

Style for Less

F ebruary is the time of year when your finances are at an all-time low. You're still sitting on all your bills from the holidays and you're in a funk, but the one thing that *could* cheer you up (a fast injection of new fashion splurges) is not going to get you out of the red. So it is a good time to consider your budget options. Ready for the challenge? Can you be the queen of cheap as well as chic? You betcha! And if poverty is the mother of all invention, February is the month to give birth to a new habit of frequenting thrift and budget stores.

TOOLS FOR BUDGET STYLE

Putting together a stylish look on a budget requires a few key pointers. Once learned, these will soon become an automatic and integral part of your daily dressing. Budget style is about lifestyle just as much as price tags.

If "budget style" is not already in your fashion lexicon, it most definitely should be! But first, let's define budget style. For some, it is the purchase of anything under $500. For others, it may be something scoured at a garage sale for 10 cents (and worn fabulously with a Gucci outfit). For others it may mean *anything* on sale under $10.

Ten hot habits of successful budget-style shoppers

No matter how you grade your levels of budget style, there are some general principles that can apply to us all in an effort to get started.

1. **Go window-shopping!** Why? Well, for a start, it's not always possible to go out on a shopping trip and purchase exactly what you had in mind. Clothes shopping is not an exact science; it's a combination of there being stock in the stores carrying what you want and finding items there that inspire and fit your body and budget. Quite a few factors have to come into alignment before you pick out a perfect item. So consider the trips where you don't find exactly what you want right away simply "research" trips. Time spent out cruising the stores is valuable. You pick up information about what's out there, and moreover, once you've tried on many items that don't suit you, you gradually learn what doesn't work. In addition, time spent window-shopping—either by literally looking in windows or by actually trying on things and not buying them—is great for honing your radar for bargain finds. Constantly exposing yourself to luxury fashion items means that your eye can more easily pick out a bargain-priced piece that looks expensive. Your radar for honing in on it is more finely tuned.

2. **Shop a little here and there.** Just as Rome wasn't built in a day, your bargain hunting doesn't (and shouldn't!) happen in the same shopping trip. Sometimes it's even more gratifying when it doesn't. Making multiple trips is a

great way for you to acquire the pieces as you see them rather than all at once in a frantic search. You may see one item on your lunch break, another great piece on Saturday afternoon after your manicure, and a third you're not sure about but might revisit if it's still there on the weekend. It may be a difficult adjustment at first, but it'll pay off! The day you see the perfect shoes at the right price to go with that awesome dress you practically stole for next to nothing may just be the day you needed a pick-me-up anyway. It'll be *so* much fun piecing them together at home.

3. Shop online. The computer really can be an advantage even if you're not much of an e-commerce person. Many fashion insiders do need and enjoy the touchy-feely experience of shopping in an actual store where the merchandise is and not in cyberspace, but it's still great for comparing prices and seeing what's available before you go. This kind of preparation saves times so it's still budgeting even if it's only on time. Clichéd though it is, time is money when you are busy, so click on! Look things up on eBay. It's a great place to shop for things you *know* about. If you know a certain designer's clothes and you know they fit you well and they are always, always the same size, see if there is anything from the designer's collections available on eBay or other online auction sites.

You can also use the computer to shop online for overstock or sales from your favorite retailers that you normally shop in person. Stores that are solely online often have no massive overhead like rent and employees and can offer great bargains. Just read the sales policy of any site thoroughly to be sure you can make easy returns.

4. Mix high and low fashion. Do seek out some big name luxury designer items or accessories because mixing high fashion with low is one of the coolest, smartest ways to style a unique outfit. The key is to source a few pieces of designer clothing or accessories, whether or not purchased new or used, and pair them with budget finds. The key lies in the quality of the high-end pieces. They immediately upgrade everything they're worn with. Wearing just one piece of luxury designer clothing or an accessory per outfit is a good ratio. But if you're crafty, you can substitute a unique one-of-a-kind piece from an unknown designer for a luxury designer one. Either way, you certainly don't need to pay full price for these special items! It's called raising the fashion bar. If you *build* your look starting with just one special piece of quality high-end designer clothing or a unique accessory, this is a most effective budget-style habit. It's not necessary to pay full retail for a designer item, there are plenty of consignment stores out there that carry items from past seasons and quality lightly used designer goods. And of course, if you're really lucky and sharp, you might even grab a designer bargain from the thrift store or find a truly unique vintage item that has no label but is clearly of exceptional quality.

The idea is to choose an item that is exceptional on you. Take, for example, a pair of large, splashy classic Kenneth Jay Lane costume jewelry earrings or a vintage Gucci bag from an antiques fair. These are unique collector's items and could even be at the top end of your budget. However, it is their "quality" factor that you are going for. And this makes them pair so well with a fresh white shirt and new pair of jeans from a lower-priced high-fashion retailer like H&M or a department store like JCPenney—and you will still have some left over for a visit to fabulous discount shoe emporiums like DSW or Famous Footwear for the trend shoe of the season. Similarly, you could pair the lower-priced jeans and white shirt with shiny brand-new quality designer items like Dior sunglasses or a Marc by Marc Jacobs jacket and transform the whole look. This is how you *keep* under budget. The overall effect is one of luxury, but the reality is that the majority of the outfit is sourced as budget finds. This method even holds true for workout wear. Splurge on your favorite brand name sneakers; then go pick out fresh sweats, hoodies, and tees to complement them from an outlet store.

5. Repeat good successful shopping places and patterns. Find cheap stores and outlets and keep on returning regularly or go whenever they get their new shipments. My mom is the queen of this, and that's how it became ingrained in me. She'll go back to the store every day until her tenacity pays off and she returns home with the item she wants in her size. If you're not sure of when the shipments come in, ask a store employee; that person should be happy to tell you. But you have to keep on top of things. The discount merchandise in fast-sell fashion stores is hot off the rails, has a high turnover, and won't last long. Fast-fashion stores stock trendy things, and the idea is to sell them quickly while the trend is still hot. There is a reason H&M restocks every day. They need to! Other savvy shoppers will snap up your bargains, so you have to be in it to win it (the store that is). But with a practiced eye, you can quickly scan your regular favorite store in a few minutes and determine if there's anything new or worth trying on. Returning armed with this knowledge will save you huge chunks of time because you won't be searching endlessly through last week's stock that you've already seen.

6. Ignore all size tags—the fit is all. Look for your size, but don't avoid trying on a size below or two sizes above you. You can skimp on quality and even a designer name if the damn thing fits you—*really fits you.* Who *cares* what the label says the size is if it fits like magic? You can always cut the label out once you get it home! The same jacket in two different sizes can give you a completely different look, so ignore the size tag and go with what feels the best.

7. Look in unexpected places. Don't skip over the boys department, girls department, and men's or even "tweens" department (that's midway between girls and teenagers) in the big department stores. All these places can be good hunting grounds, especially if you're petite or tall. Just because you're not a tween or are on the more mature side of thirty, the tween department or a tween-dedicated store can stock fun jackets, scarves, sweaters, and tees that can be teamed with your more grown-up stuff. Don't doubt it; just try it on!—and you'll see what I mean. This isn't an excuse to end up looking like Britney Spears' tackier older sister, so please, *please* avoid glitter and cartoon motifs. But young prints, colors, and cuts can flatter if paired with more conservative neutrals and designer jeans. Tween stores do so much business in tees, whether long or short, cropped, cap sleeved, or deconstructed. It's really worth taking a look. Sometimes these items might just work well layered, so they needn't fit as the designer intended on a teenager with a flat stomach. And once again, check your size reservations at the door. Remember, you can buy any size for yourself just as long as you can make it look good.

8. Store less-expensive items just as you would higher-priced items (or they really won't last). If you take care of that beaded $25 sweater in the same way as you do your precious cashmere cardigans, they'll serve you almost as long. Hand wash them carefully if you prefer to skip the dry cleaners, and fold them carefully so they don't stretch out on hangers.

9. Ask about returns. In case you are in an indecisive mood and just don't know whether that pleather pocketbook really screams "Marc Jacobs influence" or "moment of bad shopping judgment," ask about the return policy and make sure you're cool with it. It's no good getting something for less if you are not 100 percent sure about it and it can't go back. That's throwing money away.

10. Remember, just try it on! This is the bottom line of course, and always will be. That item ticketed at $15.99 could just be *your* proportions, be *your* color, and make *you* look like a million bucks. If you try it on and it looks fabulous, you'll get that tingle of excitement and you'll just know. Your fellow shoppers will stare or comment on how well you look. Snap it up, but try it on first.

NB: A note on the concept of paying full retail: Many fashion editors do swear by *not* paying full retail for anything, but I don't. It's not realistic for normal women with busy lives. Fashion editors' lives revolve around fashion, and so their opportunities to acquire items are mul-

Style File

Making fewer purchases overall is in its own right a habit of budget style. You can do this by creating what designers would call a "capsule collection." This is essentially a smaller number of very versatile, hardworking items that all get lots of use and pair well with each other to create multiple looks. Remember, less is more, and you will have more to spend another month.

tiplied in huge numbers. My mantra is to go shop as soon
as the stuff you want hits the stores, get exactly what you
need, no more, and stop spending right then and there.
The mix-and-match cocktail of higher-priced and lower-
budget items after that is up to you.

WHAT TO BUY BUDGET

Anything is possible in life. Even finding your heart's fashion
desires on a budget. However, as a general rule, items are
available that you can get away with paying less for and
still look great in. These are items that don't need to be
made of the very best fabrics or things that can be forgiving
in the cut.

Budget buys

Here's what you can get away with getting really cheap (and
new):

Tanks
Tees
Sweats
Trendy shoes/boots
Socks
Hose
Shirts

This list can also include trend-led high-fashion items (yes,
that includes ponchos, fringed thingies, leggings, or anything
you may wear this season and never again). It can include
anything in black, because black covers a multitude of sins.
Bear in mind that this does not mean you skimp on buying
quality items in black as it is also the color on which to

splurge. Lower-priced sweaters are trickier items, but occasionally, when the fit and embellishment and textile quality are right, they are a real *find*.

Budget busts

Of course, rules are meant to be broken, and if you search carefully, you can find great budget skirts and jeans and even a jacket or two to add to the list once in a while. But in general, skip scrimping on the following:

Suits
Pants
Fitted jackets
Coats

Basically, anything really tailored is much harder to find new and on the cheap without *looking* really cheap. Vintage and thrift store finds, of course, are different. Be wary of super shiny things, loud prints, and animal prints. But use your judgment as the situation calls.

Style File

When it comes to jeans, it's all about the best cut, so splurge for these if you want the best look!

Better buys

The middle ground is pocketbooks, *some* jeans, some classic shoes, and some dresses for both summer and winter. These can, in some cases, be found on the cheap and look like a million bucks. It depends on the fabric, the cut, and, of course, your particular shape.

HOW AND WHAT TO BUY AT THE THRIFT STORE OR FLEA MARKET

Okay, either you'll be into this or you won't. Some people won't go near a thrift store or a flea market for budget shopping. They get wigged out about buying used clothes. While you don't *need* to comb these haunts for old stuff, why miss out on a potentially once-in-a-lifetime fashion find by being squeamish? You can always limit yourself to accessories. Shopping a thrift store or flea market is definitely a special kind of outing. It's not the kind of browsing you can do on the way home from work laden with groceries. It takes a certain amount of special preparation. But once you've gotten the hang of it, it should become second nature. And, hopefully, your success rate for fabulous finds will improve with practice! So here are a few pointers to get ready for the fashion budget battle!

* *Please go thrift store shopping wearing flat shoes.* If you have a small bag with a long strap that you can wear diagonally across your body, messenger bag style, use it. Take no pocketbook. You need both hands to rummage properly. Ideally, go with a girlfriend for backup. That velvet-trimmed jacket with peacock feathers may scream YSL to you but, your pal may bring you back to life and give you a "Three Musketeers thumbs-down."

* *Keep all your objective opinions near the surface here, please.* It's very easy to be swayed by fairly good *almost right* stuff. Don't buy anything that doesn't blow you away.

* *Don't search for anything in particular.* Never source something directly, like, "I *gotta* get a dress for tonight." Thrift finds don't happen like that (unless you

have magical powers), and often items need time for some TLC such as dry cleaning and mending before you can wear them anyhow. When it comes to second-hand shopping, slow down and take your time, and good things will come to you. That's the karma of thrift shopping!

✳ *Feel your way around—literally.* Glide down the aisles, letting your hand slowly pass over each of the hangers and think about what you are feeling more than what you are looking at. You know how a rich or quality fabric feels, so let your sense of touch guide you. When your fingers stumble on a luxurious or unusual textile, pull it out, assess the style, the shape, the size, the condition, and the *smell* of the piece.

✳ *Don't discriminate.* When browsing thrift stores or flea markets, don't discriminate. Just because you never heard of the designer or there is no label, doesn't mean it isn't a find. Especially if it's old. There's no point going to the thrift store with your regular snob label values in place. Decades ago regular clothes were often made with much more care than they are today, so even if it's not a designer label, it can still be of very high quality. If you find a recent piece from a current designer you know and like, hang on to it for dear life! The thrift store is a designer cast-off graveyard and things can be resurrected.

✳ *Don't be a fabric snob either.* Some funky sixties fabrics were a little out there, but they are still fun pieces to mix.

✳ *Re-assess at the end of each aisle when you're done browsing.* Don't, don't put anything down. Flea and thrift buyers are a mix of clueless and savvy. Someone could see you stylishly wending your way up the aisles and hope that your flair and luck will rub off on them. They'll deliberately pick up your castoffs. This is another good reason to shop in pairs. One holds the loot while the other tries and buys.

Always think about the price. Obviously, coats or vintage evening gowns will be more (think up to $100 or more for a vintage coat), but as a rule of thumb, thrift buys must not cost more than the same category of items at discount retailers unless they are high-end designer castoffs. Remember that prices vary across the country. Thrift stores in LA near Beverly Hills or Palm Beach are likely to have great designer consignments, but prices are likely to be higher too. Country thrift stores often have better stocks than city ones since they have less traffic, so make a detour on that road trip!

✻ *Don't appear too keen on any item.* This is *especially* true if you are at the flea market. If you can fake it (not letting on about your excitement of potentially buying) and can barter a little, it can't hurt!

WHEN TO SPLURGE

Buying something expensive is a little like picking out a new car. Splurging on a designer item, be it a black dress or important pair of long leather boots that will last for years or even a terrific watch, is a bit stressful. Before you splurge, consider your options carefully. What will truly give you lasting wear and satisfaction? Also consider your lifestyle and the climate you live in, your home pet-hair situation (no, seriously!), and your bank balance. There is really no long-lasting joy to owning that new sweater if you can't feed your kids for two weeks. In fashion editor speak, splurges

❋ ❋ ❋ ❋ ❋ ❋ ❋ ❋ ❋ ❋ ❋ ❋ ❋ ❋ ❋ ❋ ❋

Eight Rules for Effective Thrift Store Shopping

So you've found a piece of secondhand clothing that you like. And it fits! But should you buy it? Here is a checklist to run in your mind:

1. Smell it. Maybe it's never been worn and is fresh as a daisy. But if it's not, ask yourself "Can it be washed?"

2. Check to see if it's the shape or length or style you'd wear and if the condition is perfect; then ask yourself, "Can it be altered or mended?"

3. Make sure that if you want to alter it you can figure out how you would alter it immediately while you are standing right there, or pass on it.

4. Choose whatever you want, be it jewelry or a pocketbook or shoes (my favorite flea and thrift buys), but just try it on!

5. Make up your mind. Do you love the item? Really love it like *love at first sight* love it? Would you buy it if it were full price and new in a store? The answer should be a resounding yes! If it's not, walk away.

are called "investment items." Whatever you choose to call them, they may not be great investments if the shocking colors do not flatter you or the cut is wrong for your figure. However, depending on your style, a splurge on a pink coat or red bag could be your serious signature item for years to come, so don't be so safe that you forget to be stylish when you splurge.

✳ ✳ ✳ ✳ ✳ ✳ ✳ ✳ ✳ ✳ ✳ ✳ ✳ ✳ ✳ ✳ ✳

6. *Do not put it down* if you really love something. Someone else will pick it up and all your hard searching will be lost! Is it a bargain? A thrift buy *must* be a bargain. If it needs alterations, could you do them yourself? (Some funky things look great with a salvage or raw hem showing anyway.)

7. Examine your finds *very* carefully while you wait to pay. It's your last chance to bail. Also, if the items are still great but more damaged than you first saw, sometimes you can get further reductions.

8. Set a budget to your budget shopping. If the budget for the thrift stores outing is $40 and your fashion finds total $42.99, get them. But $52 is not $42. Stick to your guns. Don't underestimate the cost of renovating or altering an item. You must get your math whiz head on while thinking over buys that will need attention. Obviously, something that requires a quick wash and a snip of the scissor or fresh buttons (which you know you can easily source and sew on yourself) won't count. Some tailor alterations are pricey, so be sure you really think hard about buying something that needs serious work.

Style File

As a rule of thumb, any splurges on coats, good leather shoes or boots, classic pocketbooks, dresses, and suits should ideally be in neutral colors. Neutrals are forever neutral. They work with all. Long live neutrals.

Super Splurges

The following is a list of splurge-worthy items that are definitely worth a little more consideration in the dollars allowance sector:

- A number of classic silk scarves in colors you know will flatter you.

- A pair of black or brown Italian leather high-heeled boots that never go out of style each winter. If you don't live in a cold climate or don't spend enough time in the cold weather, skip these and spend on warmer-weather basics.

- An embellished pair of eveningwear-style high-heeled, strappy stiletto sandals.

- A classic leather daytime pocketbook in a neutral color.

- A classic long winter coat in black or neutral.

- A fancy or fun winter coat, in fur or with other faux fur trim.

- A pair of designer jeans that really, really flatter you.

- A long vintage evening gown (the chances of another guest wearing the same one at the same time are very, very slim).

- A designer or vintage short cocktail dress.

- A few pieces of vintage costume jewelry. (Some of the older pieces are very cool, and both an investment and a splurge!)

- A fitted designer pantsuit in neutrals.

- A few cashmere-quality sweaters or cardigans.

What to Shop in February

* Panties
* Bras
* Camis
* Hosiery
* Lingerie

February has a lot going on in terms of merchandise. There are first denims and spring cardigans as well as a few bathing suits for the spring breakers. And let's not forget about spring shoes! But the big buy this month is *underwear* and *lingerie* of all descriptions. February is all about panties, bras, hose, camis, thongs, and lingerie. This vast and varied influx of underpinnings is due to the imminent arrival of the sexiest day of the year—Valentine's Day. February is very much lingerie and underpinnings month! This entire category is called intimates by retailers and encompasses everything in your underwear drawer from front-fastening bras to fishnets. February is the moment that all the underwear trends debut, so you'll see the most exotic and prettiest pieces at this time. Even if you don't have a Mr. Right, be nice to yourself and get a fresh new set of sexy underwear this Valentine's Day.

Before you go shopping for pretty new undies, please put in the garbage anything grayed, worn, or torn, and nix anything that otherwise should have been buried a decade ago. Most importantly, update your bra collection. The right bra size can be life changing! Whether you are planning to go online to a huge site like Figleaves.com or make a pilgrimage to Victoria's Secret, pay careful attention to how the bras fit you. In general, the center front should lie flat against the body, and there should never be a gap between the cups and the breast. Shoulder straps should not dig in because most of the support of a well-fitting bra should come from the band around the ribcage, and this band should ideally stay horizontal all the way around. No wires should dig into any breast tissue, anywhere. When you try on the bra, lift up your arms to be sure that the back does not ride up and to double-check that the wire in front stays in place. Finally, avoid trying on bras when you have your period as your size could be different.

Don't forget the purpose of the bras you splurge on either. T-shirts look tacky and ridiculous worn with a lacy bra underneath. So if you live in jeans and tees, be smart and get T-shirt-friendly soft cup bras. But don't pass up the opportunity to pick up a fresh lacy number whether its underwire or balcony style or just frivolously flirty to feel sexy, anytime, anywhere. Owning a stellar set of matching bra and panties is a fast and feminine fashion fix for the February blahs.

PS: If you spent the first half of February waiting to see if you *might* get some lingerie as a gift from a special *him* on Valentine's Day and are disappointed, don't fret. Lovely lingerie leftovers are just as fabulous on February 15th as they were on the 14th, only cheaper, as they'll probably go on sale.

Jo Jeffery, who is a spokesperson for the award-winning (and world's largest) branded intimates website at Figleaves.com always points out that most of us reach to put on the same ten pieces of underwear each laundry cycle. So it makes sense to recognize what you like and what is comfortable. You know the style you wear most, so be savvy and get what you use most.

TIPS FOR A LOWER TAB

One of the smartest tips for a lower tab when it comes to underwear is to be creative in the mix and match arena. If you buy yourself a luxury new bra you needn't always stick to the same brand to match up the panties to make a set. Chances are that cheaper brand thongs in a three-pack in the same color from a discount department store are a more realistic way to get use from your gorgeous bra more often. A bra doesn't need washing every day, if you match it closely in color with a three-pack of thongs, you can stretch it out half the week!

PS: Don't forget to hand wash that gorgeous bra to extend its life even further and get more from your pennies than you thought possible. And never, ever tumble dry a luxury lacy gorgeous bra. It will ruin it immediately! Enjoy wearing your laciest hottest undies throughout the coldest stretch of winter because soon it will be spring and tees and tanks will be back and T-shirt bras will rule again.

As February draws to a close, hopefully you will have rethought your views on thrift shopping and will have maybe even tried it out for yourself. The great thing about thrift shopping is that it does not adhere to the seasonal merchandising calendar and always depends on the good luck and timing of donations. Of course, you can practice your thrift shopping skills anytime during the year, and with these new skills, you will always be able to quench your desire for shopping anytime, anywhere in the country. But with March right around the corner and a hint of spring in the air, you can be truly thrifty and not spend much at all in February. You might want to save for a splurge on designer-name sunglasses ready to greet the sun.

* MARCH *

The Coolest Shades

*Y*eah! The sun is finally trying to come out after that long dragging winter. And once we hit the spring solstice, the days will get lighter and brighter. So it's time for you to make a note to yourself: get shades. But not just any pair. These special and sometimes spectacular accessories can make or break your outfits. They can improve and put the groove in your mood, and if not chosen wisely, they will hurt your pocketbook without sufficiently earning their keep. No one accessory can change your attitude as quickly (well, maybe killer heels), but sunglasses are certainly quick and super interchangeable. It's so darn easy to go from pretty and preppy to moody and cool in one quick change. The trick is not only to own a small stable of styles to have at the ready, but also to own *only* the right shades for you—so you make 'em all count!

Maybe you've never noticed before, but around every March, the new styles of shades hit the stores. It's as if every New Year, a new vintage of sunglasses is born! Quite often shades are closely linked to runway trends and regular fashion trends, but sometimes they take on a life of their own for other reasons. Hollywood plays a big part in all this. A new hit movie with a character who swaggers around in a memorable pair of shades is just as likely to influence the styles of shades (and your desire to have them) as a retro groovy hit music video does. Movies are just fab at spawning annual fashion trends. And if there's a big trend afoot that jumps out from the movies, it's usually the most visible at this time of year because the Oscars always happen in late February or early March.

But no matter *how* you get the influences that guide your sunglass preferences, and even if you are just bursting to have the hit thing of the moment, one thing you have to take into account before you open your wallet: your face shape. You wouldn't go shopping for a pair of shoes without knowing your size, right? It's the same with sunglasses and the shape of your face. The cool part is that face shape is one thing about you (like your shoe size) that doesn't change much, so your investment in

Style Note

When choosing sunglasses, pick a shape that contrasts with your face. This is basic design and balance sense and style karma! If you've got a round face, get some angles. If you're square, get some curves. It's all about face flattery.

cool shades will be relevant long after your waistline and or hips expand and shrink and expand back again.

LEARN THE SCIENCE OF SUNGLASSES

Okay, the form-meeting-function thing may not be exactly what you expect to read here. But just in case you might be thinking of skipping out on quality shades, scan this quickly so you can feel justified and satisfied that you've made a worthwhile investment. You've heard of the Earth's depleting ozone layer, right? Well, as much as this is an environmental problem, it also means increased UV radiation reaches our eyes, which isn't good at all. Thankfully, the best, most healthful and most stylish antidote is to get shades that are rated to block 99–100 percent of both UVA and UVB rays. Sunnies (that's the Australian slang for shades, what a great word!) aren't just for those sparkling summer days—you should be wearing them all year long. Sunlight is the primary source of UV radiation that damages the eyes and causes premature aging, since the skin around the eyes is supersensitive and is easily harmed. Without boring you with a lot of science, *just get the right shades* if you want to stave off age-related macular degeneration (accelerated aging of the retina), skin cancer (10 percent of which occurs *on* the eyelids), or cataracts (blurry vision caused by the eye's lens getting cloudy). The right shades filter out 99–100 percent of UVA and UVB, and they are marked as such when purchased from a reputable eyewear boutique or department store.

But it's just as important to pick shades according to your lifestyle. Different lenses offer different benefits, and it pays to know which do what. A smart rule of thumb is to choose at least *one* pair of shades for everyday wear and possibly *two* others that work specifically just for fashion, driving, or outdoor activities. If you pick carefully, your stable of shades will grow steadily. Make one new purchase each year, and you'll end up with a mighty cool collection. If you know your sun science, you'll make wise purchases that will fill gaps in your sunglass wardrobe and not make duplicates on impulse. You don't have to be a math whiz to see that this strategy ultimately saves you money.

Face-shape analysis

First, let's figure out your face. Then you can match the frame shape suggestions to it:

* A *triangle*-shaped face like Kathy Ireland's features a narrow forehead that gets wider at the cheeks and chin. A triangle looks fab in frames that are heavily accented in color on the top half or in aviator frames because these create balance.

* A *round* face like Charlize Theron's has the same measurements in both the width and the length. A round face does not have harsh angles or prominent cheekbones and, thus, looks fab in angular, narrow frames like rectangles or geometric shapes because these styles break up the monotony of a round face.

* An *oval*- or egg-shaped face like Gwen Stefani's is perfectly symmetrical and is a very easy shape to work with. It looks great in almost any style, but shields or wraparounds often look the coolest. They scream "timeless sporty cool."

* A *diamond*-shaped face like Jennifer Aniston's has high cheekbones and is narrow at the eye line and jawline. A diamond looks fab in cat-eye or square or rimless frames because these frames balance out the widest and narrowest parts of the face.

* An *oblong* face like Sarah Jessica Parker's is longer than it is wide, and often features long, straight cheekbones. An oblong looks best in frames that are deep from top to bottom or have decorative temple details. Temple details draw the eye to the middle of the head where the ears are and break up the longness of the face. Wraparounds can look good on the oblong, especially if they are deep.

* A *square* face like Cameron Diaz's has a broad forehead and a very strong jawline. Squares look fab in
  narrow frames like ovals, rounds, or cat-eye styles.
  John Lennon–style round shades are classic examples
  here, but cat-eye shapes are much sexier.

* A *heart-shaped* face like Reese Witherspoon's has a
  very wide top and tapers down to a narrow chin or a
  small bottom. Hearts look fab in frames that gradually
  get wider toward the bottom closer to the cheekbones
  and are narrower on top closer to the eyebrows. Any
  light or rimless shades flatter well too.

KNOW YOUR LENSES

Where you will *wear* your shades will determine the kinds
of lenses and tints that you should choose.

Here's the scoop on lens types:

Photochromatic lenses automatically darken and
lighten depending on where you are, so these
lenses are super flexible and adjust when moving
from indoors to outdoors. They are very good all
around for city living, indoor and outdoor activities,
and computer work. The lenses may not darken as
much as you want, or at all, when in a car or bus
because of the tinted windshield or windows.
This technical feature is very useful if you are
constantly on the move.

Polarized lenses filter out glare and shine from
water and keep the contrast good so they reduce
squinting and eyestrain. These are great if you
are going to be doing a lot of driving or outdoor
activities such as boating.

Picking Sassy Styles

Nothing is worse than sunglasses that don't fit. They won't protect your eyes, they'll take the edgy cool off your greatest outfits, and they'll just never work for you—even if you change your hair.

DON'T BUY:

- Anything that is too small or that does not protect your eyes. Tip: lenses that touch your eyelashes are too close for your face.

- Anything that is too big. Tip: deep shades that hit your cheekbones or are much wider than the width of your face are too big for you.

DO BUY:

- Shades that fit. The glasses should not allow light to creep in from the top, sides, or underneath. And well-fitting shades should never hit your cheeks, your eyelashes, or your face anywhere except the bridge of the nose on which they sit.

- Shades with plastic arms. This is especially helpful if you know you will wear them pushed up on your hair to go indoors a lot, as plastic causes less hair breakage than metal does.

- Spray cleaner and a soft cloth to keep your shades clean and hygienic when ready to store them in their case.

Impact-resistant or tempered lenses are fortified! No, they have not eaten their Wheaties, but they are superstrong and are very good for beach sports, snow sports, and the outdoors in general.

Antireflective lenses reduce glare, which makes eyes more comfortable in odd lighting situations. That's why these are the best if you live and breathe for driving your car, riding your bike, or walking outside.

Flash mirrors cut down on light entering the eyes, which means comfortable eyes. Period. They are a key choice for beach or water sports. They just happen to look ultra sporty, sleek, and futuristic too.

Gradients cut glare because they provide gradual shading from the top down or bottom up. They also make you look wonderfully mysterious!

Brand buzz

Once you've figured out where you will want to wear your shades, you can finally hone in on your favorite brands.

When you start looking at fashion brands of sunglasses, think of them as fashion for your face. For example, a pair of Kate Spades may add a much-needed touch of preppy cuteness if you're a Rocker Chick at heart. Likewise, if you're normally an uptown Glamourpuss and you try out a pair of grunge-friendly Marc Jacobs shades, you'll likely acquire some downtown cool. Of course, this can be a great thing. If you want to add some instant provocative energy to your look, try on some Alexander McQueens! If you're in the mood to channel some movie star magic, try on Gucci

Color Me Right

To round out your sun science 101, take into account which lens colors work best for which activity. Some are more desirable than others are in a practical way (not just a fashion way!)

Yellows work great outdoors and driving, and they give great depth perception in low light.

Pinks work great in the snow, at the beach, or on the road for driving because they improve color perception in low light or overcast weather.

Greens work great for work at the computer and for everyday use because they enhance contrast in moderate light and reduce eyestrain in bright conditions.

Browns and ambers work great for reducing glare and minimizing eyestrain by improving contrast. These are fab for outdoor sports and driving.

Grays work great for most outdoor pursuits and for driving and sports. They evenly transmit true colors that reduce distortion and glare.

for a hint of glamour. No item allows you to change up your persona more quickly than sunglasses.

Where you go to buy your shades is important. In general, I recommend eyewear-specific boutiques as the best sunglass-shopping spots. Department stores carry great batches of sunglasses, but they aren't always as easy to try on, and the atmosphere can be distracting. Moreover, a good sunglass store will let you briefly step out into the daylight with your chosen shades on for a quick test. You really can't do this in a department store. A wonderful store to check out is the Solstice Sunglass Boutique. This specialty store is filled with designer brands and with lots of accessible mirrors, and better still, the sunglasses are not stashed behind scary glass cases! But no matter where you go, try to find a place that makes it easy to try on glasses and that sells brands made by well-known manufacturers who test for UV protection.

Sometimes you can find what you want online or on eBay, but of course you may not get the guarantee that the shades you pick aren't scratched or that they're 100 percent authentic. And of course, you can't try them on until it's too late, so be sure you know what you're buying. Going on eBay is a great place for sunglass shopping only if you know exactly what you want, which style number, and which brand and only if you have tried those glasses on before. Perhaps a friend owns them. But when you buy over the Internet, you have to remember that unless you can see the label of authenticity, you can

Style File: When to Break the Rules a Little

Once in a while, a pair of shades comes along that takes your fancy—that just screams *you*—even if it isn't the perfect style for your face shape. Just get them! Life is too short, and you should always have a pair of shades that you love!

be taking a chance that they're the real thing and that the site will protect you as you would want. Also, be sure you can live with the return policy. And what about saving money and buying cheaper copycat shades from a street or market vendor? Here's the fashion insider's take: If you've already picked up a cheapo *backup* pair to throw into your F.E.K. or into your purse and are worry free about scratches, keep the glasses for just that—backup. Don't buy any new pairs this way. The cheapo price of these backup sunglasses usually means they won't protect your eyes *at all* from UV light.

DEVELOP SHADES SENSE

Since sunglasses are the accessory worn right up close to your hairstyle, it's really crucial that they suit each other. Brad Johns, my hair guru and hair color director at the Elizabeth Arden Red Door Salon & Spa in New York, taught me long ago that hair color is the one accessory that you don't take off. He says, "When you're naked at the end of the day, it's you, your bod, and your hair color!" And he's right.

And although Brad always preached that hair should *never* be the color of vegetables or foods, your sunglasses *can* be these colors and they often accent really nicely. However, just because you love jet-black Jackie O oversized Diors does not mean that they are *always* a good match for your hair. Sometimes a more subtle tortoiseshell can be less jarring. Brad's shade-sense advice is (pardon the pun!) illuminating:

* ✳ For a striking and stylish look, you should pick shades that contrast most with your hair color.

* ✳ For a subtle, classic, or conservative look, your hair color style should blend or be closer in color and tone with your shades.

Look up your hair color and sunglass best matches in the following:

Mid-tone brunettes look great in tortoiseshell frames since all these colors are in their hair already. However, there's nothing more fab than white glasses on mid-tone brunettes, they're just so striking.

Chestnut brown brunettes look great in caramel frames.

Ashy blondes look great in frames that blend with cold color tones like silvers or blues or grays. To go against type, you should really have a ball and buy frames in red, yellow, or orange.

White blondes look great in red frames, but other safe choices are black or white as they are essentially color-less.

Golden blondes look great in frames the color of white gold. Blue or silver are also a great contrast because cold colors contrast with gold, which is warm.

Strawberry blondes and Redheads look great in green shades. It's the opposite side of the color spectrum, and it's a really intense look. For a less bold look, gold or brown works too.

Auburns look great in woodsy, maroon, burgundy, and chocolate colors but don't look that good in pure red.

LEARNING HAIR AND SHADES FROM Q&A

Still not 100 percent clear on how to pick the perfect pair? Don't panic. Here are some common solutions to the problem of finding the most stylish and suitable sunglasses, especially if you are forever changing the way you wear your hair.

Q: Who should wear metallics?
A: Well, metallics are more about where you're going than which hair shade you're currently sporting. Metallics are great for hitting the clubs on the weekend, but they're

not so great for the doctor's office or a casual Saturday brunch. It's generally better to oppose your hair color with metallics. So, if you have gold-colored hair or highlights, wear cold color metals like silver or platinum. The opposite is true if you have a colder hair color and are a dark brunette; then you should get warm gold-framed shades.

Q: *What shades should I wear with short hair?*

A: Just remember, the bigger the glasses and the shorter the hair, the more of a statement you will make. If you have short hair and do not want to make a big statement, get conservative sunglasses—not too big, not too small, and not too crazily colored. Try soft ovals or wire frames to be understated.

Q: *What shades should I wear with longer hair?*

A: The smaller the glasses and the longer the hair, the sillier you will look. Take note! The size of the shades and the length of your hair should be in agreement. You want to look sexy, confident, put together, and modern, so adjust your frame size to your hair length. If you have very short bangs framing your face but very long hair, go for large glasses. The small ones will look ridiculous. If you have a cropped haircut or any hairstyle that is only a couple of inches long, supersized frames can be overwhelming—so beware.

Q: *Will changing my hair so much affect the type of shades I pick?*

A: Hair up exaggerates your face shape, so be sure you have the correct shape-opposing sunglasses. And always bear in mind that hair at the beach, a prime place for wearing your sunglasses, looks different from hair in the city. So if your hair is naturally straight and you wear it that way consistently, you can probably get away with lots of different shapes. However, if you have natural waves or curls and you wear it blown straight some of the time and curly the rest of the time, consider that a change in hair texture and volume will change how your sunglasses will look. If your hair is bigger and fluffier at the beach, you should consider picking a slightly larger frame to compensate.

WHAT TO SHOP IN MARCH

* Sunglasses
* Denims
* Special-occasion dresses
* Spring shoes

Now it's time for a quick assessment. Pull out all your sunglasses, and referring back to the shape, lens, and color sections in this chapter, think carefully about what they are and where you wear them. Now you can see what's missing from your stash. Perhaps you're missing a really good pair for driving or a better pair of polarized-specific shades for water sports.

But also, try to imagine what you *think* you might want to be wearing this summer from a fashion standpoint. For example, if there is a trend in revival clothing of the 1980s and you think you will look good in it, consider that retro shades rather than futuristic ones might better suit your wardrobe. In other words, think ahead of what will work with the clothes you hope to wear. If your new personal favorite Style Icon is a European actress, channel some Euro-chic glamour and styling when you shop for your shades. The choice of "hit" sunglasses each summer season is really so often etched into our minds from something influentially visual, be it a movie or a video or a cameo appearance or a commercial or other televised event. Sunglasses are the sort of accessory that we all identify with very easily, and if a clear identity is "at large" for the season, you are likely to pick it up. March is also the month when the first big spring shipments arrive. So that means denim is in full swing now, with bigger selections than the first pairs that trickled in last month, so it is a fine time to *get jeans*. It is a great time to look for pretty *special occasion dresses* for graduations, bridal showers, and weddings too. There is a continuation of earliest *spring shoe* batches now too, and if you have found your perfect sunglasses already, then it is an opportunity to pick shoes that coordinate.

TIPS FOR A LOWER TAB

Please, please, don't buy your major shades from the street vendor or a market stall. If you already have them, relegate them to the F.E.K. Don't call me a pooh-bah! Your eyes are too important and must be protected, and although some designer styles can be very pricey, there are brands that do honestly bring as much cache and protection with less scary price tags. Department stores have brands that retail for under $50. For example, JLo has a line of shades that retail at about $40–$50 and almost exactly imitates higher-end designers like Christian Dior. The quality of the plastic and durability may not last quite as long, but you'll get the same style value. Very often these shades are made in the same factory by the same folks who are making the high-end designer brands and therefore carry the safety of 100 percent

UV protection. Be creative and flexible about hunting them down and trying them on.

Be sure to check out all the brands—even if you do not normally wear their clothing. Their clothes may be too young, too trendy, or too old for you, but their eyewear could be a match. So just try them on. J Lo's clothing may not be up your alley, but a pair of her sunglasses may work just great. You may not be preppy like J. Crew, but its shades may flatter your face shape. This is a clever shopping and styling trick that veteran stylist Laurie Schechter calls "casting against type." You are wearing something you thought you would not ever wear. But the contrast on you really works. Simple as that. And in this instance, it could save you a stash of cash.

Ever heard of Swapsies? Probably not as I made it up! It's my word for getting together with a group of good friends or your sisters and throwing a sunglass party. Tell them to bring a couple of pairs of shades that they are tired of and wouldn't mind passing on; then have a big shade swap. If everyone plays fair and brings quality stuff, it's very possible that someone else will look good in your shades, and vice versa. If you and your posse of friends are real fashion hounds and already have a dozen past pairs between you, this can be the ultimate fashion fix. It's one of the coolest forms of fashion recycling.

So, as March comes to a close, you should be armed with a newly edited collection of sunglasses and ready-to-make super-smart choices on future purchases to coordinate with your everyday style. Fabulous new shades paired with other early spring purchases like shoes or jeans will mean that you're getting set to face the lengthening days. And although slightly longer days may seem like a far cry from the dog days of summer, believe it or not, the next big category to hit the stores during early April is swimwear. Hopefully, you've budgeted to keep back a few bucks for a splashy splurge on a fab new bathing suit. It may still feel like the bitter cold midwinter, but the spring and summer shopping starts to heat up right now.

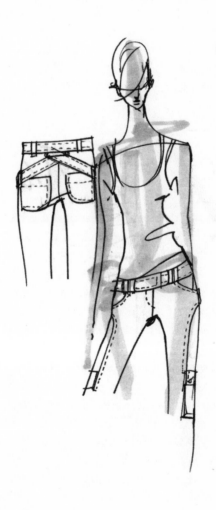

* APRIL *

Squirm-Free Swimwear

pril Fools' Day may be a joke to some, but nowhere near as bad a joke as the idea of bathing suit shopping in the cold. The very suggestion of getting deep into the bathing suit horrors in April, while we all feel pasty and are still bundled up for the colder winter, is plain off-putting. However, believe it or not, April, the early cusp of spring, is quite honestly one of the *best* times to face this fashion dilemma. I know it's no consolation if you live in a part of the country where April still feels like the middle of winter, but the truth is, countrywide, this is the time to think *beach*. The big reason is this: The bathing suit selection is the best just as April turns the seasonal corner, and if you shop now, you'll have the advantage of a wide range of size, style, and availability—and therefore a much higher chance of finding the perfect suit. If you wait until the weather warms up, your selection will be greatly diminished. It's really a numbers game. As the weeks and months go by, the availability of size and color options will drop off, leaving you with fewer choices. It's just that simple. Also, if you do make a purchase from a store to which you can return swimwear (take note, many stores *don't* take intimate returns), then at least you have the option to try it on again at home. And if you change your mind and think it's a dud on you, there's still time to return it and find a replacement from the pick of the crop.

WHERE YOU GO AND WHAT THEY KNOW

Bathing suit shopping is definitely a destination shopping excursion. By this I mean, you plan, you go, you try on swim stuff, and you don't let yourself get distracted along the way with pocketbooks, shoes, or other regalia! The key thing to remember is to pick a store or stores where you can find swimwear with the widest selection of suits because, above all, swimwear shopping, as I've said, is a numbers game. Just like kissing all those frogs to meet the prince, it's likely that you'll have to try on quite a few swimsuits to find one that really fits perfectly. If you always head to where the largest selection will be available, you won't come home empty-handed. My personal picks for choice destinations are swimwear-dedicated stores and large department stores.

Swimwear-dedicated stores

These stores are a great destination, and here's why: The sales associates will have seen each and every style on every kind of body and their knowledge is invaluable. You might pay a tad more for a suit bought at a swimwear-dedicated boutique; however, what you get in return is often the right suit that is priceless and will last you longer. Ultimately, it's time saving and budget saving. In a really good swimwear-dedicated store the sales associates can afford to be honest about how their suits look on you. This is because their personal knowledge of the store's broad selection will mean that they can offer up a *better* looking and fitting alternative when things aren't fitting well. It's also very tedious to keep dressing and perusing the suits once you're undressed. So let the sales associates really work for you.

Never underestimate the fact that swimwear styles, more than most other pieces of clothing, look much different on a body than on a rack. A good sales associate or stylist will wait and see what you pick for yourself, so let her see you in a few styles. Then if you don't like what you try on, explain what you love and don't love about those "almost" perfect suits. Here's betting that she can go back to the racks and pick alternatives you'd never have chosen for yourself that'll flatter and make you feel great. This is because she's seen the suit on previous customers. She's seen which Calvin Klein has no room for a woman with a bust, and she's seen how well the underwire in the Melissa Odabash one-piece helped a customer with a D-cup just yesterday. I know this to be true for two reasons: First, I know from my own bathing suit shopping. I hardly ever buy the suits I first choose off the racks, even though I know what suits me. Invariably a sales associate sees me in these suits and suggests something that flatters both my good and bad bits even better. Second, I know this from when I've been styling models for TV shoots. Once you've seen a particular bathing suit on a body, you can tell how forgiving or stretchy or supportive it is. After I have used the same suits for a few fashion shoots, I can practically match the model body to the best suit without her trying it on.

Department stores

Department stores are another great option for swimwear shopping, especially as the "core buy"—or what ends up on the shop floor—is much broader in the brands and styles (from grandma to teens), giving you much more to choose from. Don't limit yourself to a particular type of suit: what was designed for a more mature body might be just the cut for you. Also, you may well have the pick of the children's department if you happen to be petite or small chested, so don't forget to check this out while you are in the stores. Sales associates in department stores can be just as helpful and knowledgeable as the boutiques—as long as the store is big enough so that the swim section has its own dedicated fitting room. If it doesn't, then watch yourself! Stay focused on trying and buying swimwear not picking through dresses hanging on the holding rack. Make time for that later.

Style Note

The clues to the perfect bathing suit could be hiding right in your lingerie drawer. What's your favorite bra? What's your favorite panty? Why? Are the briefs high cut on the leg? Is the bra underwired? Look for bathing suit styles just like this when you begin shopping. You may not find the exact thing, but it's a good way to start.

Preparation tactics!

Okay, you are ready for the big day. You're actually going to go swimwear shopping at the beginning of April. How are you going to get through this without squirming? Here's how you can avoid this.

Use some kind of self-tanner. Do this a few days before you're set to shop. Even if it's only a minimal shade darker, this will make a world of difference and will make being naked so much easier. I promise!

Make sure you are having a good hair day. Do whatever it takes to make you feel good about your hair. Get it done, do it yourself, or skip the shopping today if your hair is just wrong. Though it seems like a minor detail, when you're in a changing room with just your body, a bunch of bathing suits, and your modesty, bad hair will, at worst, dampen your mood and at best distract you.

Avoid PMS at all costs. *Don't* go swimsuit shopping in the days leading up to your period. Let's just say that PMS and all its symptoms—crankiness, water retention, and so on—are the equivalent of a Molotov cocktail even for the most confident bathing suit buyer. Stay home and eat cookies that day, and don't waste your time on a fruitless shopping trip. At best you'll end up buying something that you think, hope, and pray will fit better when you're not PMSing, and at worst, you'll come away with nothing and just feel bad about your body no matter how fabulous you are. We don't want you to be totally put off about going back on another day.

Wear some makeup. Wear just enough to feel pretty so that you can smile in the mirror and be yourself instead of grimacing.

Be waxed, shaved, depilated, or all three. It's too distracting to sell yourself on a suit when the black forest is diverting your eyes to the legs, armpits, and other bits! You don't need to have a full mani-pedi and we're not talking here about getting a full spa package do-over before swimwear shopping, but it does make sense to have your bikini line under control when you go to shop for a bathing suit. You'll just feel better about yourself. Honestly.

Wear a shoe with a slight heel. This will elevate and elongate the legs a little and adjust your posture to a position of one that looks more confident—and when you look more confident, you feel more confident.

Shop alone. When shopping alone, you're forced to be brutally honest with yourself about whether you can withstand being seen in public wearing what you have tried on. A well-meaning friend or sister or mom isn't going to be wearing the suit, and any amount of bolstering or polishing up of your ego won't make you feel confident when you step out for the first time in an ill-fitting suit. I've found shopping alone for my bathing suits is the only way to get a good sense of the confidence level of each item. Don't forget, if you have befriended a good honest sales associate, she'll bring you alternative sizing and styles, so let her see you in your choices. There's no embarrassment here; she's seen everyone undressed. And I mean *everyone.* Consider her opinion because she's seen a lot of suits on a lot of

Style File

Do you have a swimsuit you once loved that's on its way to retirement? Try it on one more time, making note of the style and the brand and the size. The sizing within a brand should not change, so if you fit into a Kenneth Cole or a Jantzen suit in a medium last year and have not significantly changed your weight, then you are likely to fit a medium by the same designer this year.

bodies, and she may truly surprise you with some choices that work great for you that you'd never have picked out in a million years. However, don't be overruled by her opinion if you're truly not comfortable.

Is That a Smart Purchase?

Right. You've selected a few suits for consideration. You've gone through the whole process of finding a style that potentially fits and you like it. And then I start getting into "is that smart?" How dare I! Don't hate me for asking the question. I know it's sometimes really hard to get something you love that looks like it'll fit you. But, well, is it a smart purchase? Ask yourself the following questions.

Will it get wet?

Stupid question maybe, but not really. Some suits you just *know* are fragile. And as a result, you'll need to keep them in perfect condition so that you can lounge, look fabulous, strut around in, and wear to pool parties. The bottom line is that they're going to need to stay dry. You know these kinds of suits. They're the ones that look dressy paired with a sarong or shorts. They're the ones that are fancy enough to wear to clambakes and BBQs. These suits will likely never, nor should they ever, get wet. You can identify these kinds of suits—they're embellished with things like ribbons, have details like jewels, and are constructed of fabrics that don't do great getting wet over and over like velvet. So, that said, if you really love a suit that really fits and you don't think it can get wet, but you expect to take more than an occasional plunge this summer, bear this in mind: there's no problem having a "dry suit"; just plan your wardrobe accordingly so that you do have a "get wet" one too.

Is it white?

And therefore, is it see-through? If you have fallen in love with a white bathing suit, make sure it has a lining as this will certainly help prevent it from being see-through when it gets wet. If it *is* white and it is *not* lined and you only plan to wear it "dry" by the pool, then enjoy it.

Where will you wear it?

A gold lamé one-piece is perfect for a once-in-a-lifetime week in the south of France, not South Jersey. I don't want to burst the style bubble here, but you don't need to be a top fashion editor to think this one up. Go ahead, get the gold lamé suit if you're really going to Cannes and the suit looks great on you. If not, you can look just as sexy in something that'll work harder for you and with you and not wear *you*. If you're set on the gold bling thing, settle instead for a plainer suit, but accent with a gold sarong, gold belt, or gold thongs and jewelry. It's much classier, really.

HOW ABOUT RECYCLING SWIMWEAR?

What, you say? Recycle swimwear? *Eww, no!* Chill, I say. I mean recycle *your own* bathing suits! Here's how: Say you bought a great black bikini last year and the bottoms are now baggy and stretched out. Toss them. But hang on to that top. Especially if there is underwire in the bust and the overall look and fit is still good. You may have another black suit or a suit with black in it or a pair of bottoms that are a completely different color altogether that just match up great with it. So many new styles and designs these days are mixed and matched obtusely by design. Matchy-matchy isn't the big story in new suits anyway, so there's really no harm in keeping half a bikini that still fits for a couple of seasons until you find another top or bottom. The very cool result is that you can end up customizing your own suits that fit great—maybe even better than the original designer intentioned. Most importantly, you'll really get the maximum use and wear out of each piece no matter whether you use them for two weeks a year or whether you live in them. One spare lonely bikini halter top in the bottom of the drawer doesn't really take up that much space and could really save you later.

One-piece bathing suits are the same. Even when the bottoms are stretched out and sagging, the halter tops or wired bust areas are still going strong, so don't toss them or cut them off. They can work great paired as tops with jeans, shorts, or skirts. This isn't a license to keep every sagging suit in your drawer, but if you take an evening to try on your old stuff and think that the sexy one-piece from last season could go out on the town with a sheer blouse over it, keep it. But move it from the storage area you designated for "swim stuff" to the place where you keep your "summer tops" so that you don't think of it as swimwear anymore. That's true recycling.

So How Many Suits Do I <u>Really</u> Need?

Well, this does depend on your budget, your lifestyle (if you live in California, you'll need more bathing suits than sweaters), and how much you really think you can use them. My general rule of thumb is that for a summer season with some beach action planned, two to three suits are cool. Say you picked one you love and look lovely in it, but it's your dry suit. Then suit number two is the one that is fashionably functional and serves as your jump in the ocean "wet suit." I think everyone needs a number three. It's what I call a "spa suit" and is the kind of suit that you'll use for going into heavily chlorinated areas such as a Jacuzzi at a spa or at a public pool or for taking even a swim in the ocean where there's algae or the vague possibility of sitting on some stray staining materials on the beach. It could easily be a combination of your recyclables. Really chlorinated hot tubs wreak havoc on even the best-made bathing suits, causing them to stretch out and sag to the max. High chlorine bleaches the colors out of bathing suits too, so your third suit should essentially be the one that you don't mind being trashed but that you don't look half bad in either.

WHAT TO SHOP IN APRIL

* Bathing suits
* Skirts and pants
* Spring cardigans
* Occasion dresses
* Summer shoes and sandals

It's a big month for the summer shipments of almost everything; however, buy your *bathing suits* before anything else for the best sizes, selections, and chances of getting exactly what you want.

If you need them and can try to budget for *skirts* and *pants* during April too, then great. Spring cardigans also arrive so that if you are someone who will need long-sleeved anything in the air-conditioning of midsummer, get it now. Or perhaps a chunk of your budget must go to an *occasion dress* for a wedding? There are many gorgeous choices during this time of the year.

Buying skirts is fun. They're so easy to try on and you get to pick out colors that you can't necessarily wear near your face, which lets you expand your wardrobe a little. Say you love the color purple, but every purple shirt, sweater, or even T-shirt you've ever tried washed you out or looked drab. Well, when you buy a skirt, you can easily pick out a print that has lots of purple in it as long as it's paired with a tee or shirt that'll flatter your face. Now that you have some purple in your closet, your other accessories can work harder for you too. Any chocolate brown accessories, for example, look great with purples, and thus you have truly expanded your wardrobe options. Finding a great skirt is like finding that great bra. You can pick any number of tees or tanks in multiples to go with it. With a variety of tanks and tees on hand, you change up your outfit on the cheap.

The *summer shoes* also hit the stores in April. Keep in mind what shoes you'll be wearing with your beachwear and, if possible, take the time to window shop the luxury stores for the key trends and details of the season, as all the dressier *summer sandals* that are open toed and strappy start to arrive now. The rest of the shoe search is up to your taste, lifestyle, and budget. If you know you'll be hiking and biking and playing outdoors all summer long, with nary a wedding or bridal shower on your calendar, don't be swayed by all the gorgeous shoes. Choose one fantasy pair of evening shoes for the season. You'll know from the season's trends what's hot. If wedges are back, all the brands will do a version. If flats are in, you'll find them everywhere.

Try them all on, figure out if your ankles, legs, and feet look and feel good in the season's styles. Do not be surprised if some of the trends just miss entirely—there are always the classics to be revisited. For now, the most important thing about purchasing pretty summer shoes and sandals is to be honest about how and where you will wear them. Really high heels can be much hotter and tighter and harder to walk and stand in all day throughout the summer months, so make sure that you keep focused on getting really wearable pairs as well as your dream pairs. You can pick out one or two pairs of really great what I call "car shoes" or "limo shoes," that is, those that you won't be walking far in. Ideally, keep back some cash if you need to search for a particular pair to go perfectly with a dress you know you will purchase later.

TIPS FOR A LOWER TAB

So, your visits to the ATM might be more frequent in April than in the first several months of the year. As the weather changes, the surge of swimsuits, skirts, cardigans, and shoes all come up on the shopping agenda at pretty much the same time. But there are ways to keep tabs on your cash flow. The key here is to get *just* the suits you need and look *fab* in. If you're not a bathing beauty and don't hit the beach much, don't go overboard. It's smart to have two or three suits (including your oldest recyclable one) in your collection so that you always have a backup.

Also, remember that sometimes it's smart to spend in order to save. Do splash for the few extra dollars it may cost if you see a swimwear-specialty detergent at a bathing suit boutique. The stuff may even be pushed on you by sales staff and you may think you want to resist it, feeling like you're being suckered in to spend more. Don't fight this, buy it. In my experience, these swimwear washes are rarely more than a few dollars. They are softer, gentler detergents than regular detergents and genuinely brighten the colors while rinsing out sand or chlorine or sunscreen leftovers so that they actually protect your suits, which truly makes them last longer. I know that the last thing you want to do after a lazy day on the beach while you're prepping for a night out on the town is a careful hand rinse of your suit. But try to do it. If possible, rinse your suit as soon as you take it off with those special bathing suit suds. Follow the instructions on the bottle, and as you wash, don't scrunch the suit too much, and don't wring it, but agitate the fabric against itself. After rinsing as directed, always let your suit dry flat so it doesn't stretch out of shape. You can even roll it up in a dry towel immediately after washing to blot excess water before it is set down to dry flat. This careful treatment can really extend the life of a suit that you love, and god knows that's good news if it's taken a lot of trouble to find it in the first place, so don't skip this step if possible.

Department store prices may well be better than bathing suit-dedicated boutiques just because they buy in bulk and can carry a greater number of lower priced brands, so if you need to remain a slave to the budget, hit these *first*. However, even if you are a dedicated bathing beauty and rank your bathing suits as a top-dollar priority within your budget, buying them early whether they're the cheapest or not will ensure that you won't scrabble around trying to find multiple others later (that may be more expensive) to compensate for an unsuitable purchase.

The final tab saver is long range. The security of having your bathing suit picks already in your swimwear drawer by April means that you can keep a keener eye on what you are looking for as far as the styles, colors, themes, and details on your other clothes. This is how you add to and build on your summer capsule collection.

As far as tab-saving tips for summer shoes, again the trick is to head for a shopping destination that holds hundreds of brands in one place. But not before scouring the fancier boutiques and designer shops to see the most fabulous pairs up close and personal. The key might be to splash for one pair of more expensive designer shoes for a specific purpose (perhaps these will be your workday staple). Then you can indulge yourself with the trends by shopping the larger discount chains like DSW and Famous Footwear afterward. If you browse the high-end designer stores and kind of window shop first, you'll have a better idea of the good "imitations" available. If you're anything like I am, you'll take great glee in finding a trendy pair from a lower-priced retailer that has the same punch for much less. It's particularly satisfying! Since shoes are such a fabulous item, we sometimes get a little too passionate about them and just have to have a particular pair. You may even find a pair that is so off the wall for this summer or a pair that is so you and so amazing (even though they are hugely expensive) that you buy them and work out the new spring and summer wardrobe possibilities with them as your central focus. Like anchoring a ship at sea, all your other purchases can revolve around them. There's no harm in this. Just so long as you're sure you'll get maximum repeated wear from them.

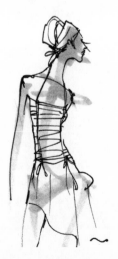

Style Icon Status

CELEBRITY STYLE

No matter what celebrities are celebrated for—be it singing, acting, or simply just being—remembering them for what they wore and how they wore it has become a huge part of our culture. Of course, since celebrities know how much their fashion sense is being watched, they definitely dress to impress. But even in light of the fact that celebrities can afford to work one-on-one with stylists who get paid to pick dresses to borrow and dress them for events that'll draw the paparazzi in droves, if a celebrity doesn't have her own personal fashion charisma, her star won't shine as bright. So, what does it take to have celebrity style? Well, there are some key points that can help you zone in on how to strengthen your personal style.

Before you begin, you will have to decide if you are a trendsetter or a style icon. There is definitely a difference. Trendsetters change their style as often as new fashions come and go. And often this might not be limited just to fashion choices or styling with accessories. It might also include other lifestyle factors such as hairstyle, body weight, or even enhancements like hair extensions. The joy of being a trendsetter is that there is always lots of flexibility. As the trends come and go, trendsetters will pick up and adapt some for themselves while steering clear of others.

Style icons, meanwhile, remain the same over time, sometimes keeping their signature looks for decades or whole lifetimes even. And there is very often some quality or feature of a style icon that remains the same over many years, sometimes even decades of fashion reincarnations. It may be an attitude or a hairstyle or a way of specifically wearing a particular fashion item. If you evolve into a true style icon, your style may well be remembered after your time is up!

The making of the modern icons

Only time will tell whether the style of our modern-day celebrities will capture the world's imagination enough for it to be recorded in the history books later on. Madonna is a perfect example of a trendsetter whose style changes with the times. On the other side, Gwen Stefani is very much a style icon. It's Gwen's forties-inspired red lipstick and Rasta-farian rocker-chic combination that somehow shines through whether or not she's in a wedding dress or sweats. One can imagine that even when she's not wearing her trademark red lipstick, she still has a 1940s posture—a self-assurance and glamorous demeanor that screen icons of the 1940s had. She owns her look. And it's unique and constant. A celebrity such as Kate Moss is harder to categorize because although her look is very trendsetting and age specific (sort of stuck in her twenties), she's both a trendsetter and an icon at the same time. What she wears often sets off trends yet adheres to her trademark twenty-something grunge look.

As a rule, there are more trendsetters than style icons,

especially among modern-day celebrities. It remains to be seen whose styles will stick and whose will sink after their time is up!

HOW TO CREATE ICONIC STYLE FOR YOURSELF

All the best icons in fashion are women with a very specific look. For example, Audrey Hepburn always wore ballet flats, tight Capris, feminine tight sweater sets, and cropped hair. These three fashion features have practically become synonymous with her name. Similarly, we all know Jackie O championed the sheath dress, imitation and real pearls, and those unforgettable oversized sunglasses, which have become iconic in their own right. Paired even with the latest trends, oversized shades *still* pay homage to Jackie O. But here's the thing: just because we know and love Jackie for those fab shades, does it mean we go right out there and copy her dress, pearls, and sunglass combinations? Sadly, it's not as easy as that. People often make this mistake, and rather than capturing their own sort of iconic styles, they wind up looking like a Jackie O imitator. The same goes for copying trendsetters. If you style your hair just like Gwen Stefani or wear Ugg boots with the same ripped denim miniskirt as Sienna Miller, you'll look more like a clone than an original. Sorry!

Style Note

If you're going for style icon status, you'll have to make yourself immune to trends. Make sure that this approach won't make you bored! You can get away with carrying a trendy accessory, but it should blend in seamlessly with your individual look so that it's barely noticeable.

So how do you recreate vintage or create iconic style for yourself?

Stick to consistency and more consistency

By repeating the same fashion element (or elements) over and over, you will *own* your own look. This is how icons become known for their style—they make a certain element a permanent part of their signature style. Whether it's part of your beauty routine or your makeup, your edgy cool eyeglasses, your hair, or your accessories, just keep something the same all the time. It could simply be that you just always, always, always wear flats, which, incidentally, is a really good tip for a very tall girl. It need only be one item or feature that remains the same. Oversized glasses personified Jackie O. What personifies *you?*

Pick a decade and a time of day

My friend Syl Tang, the founder and CEO of HipGuide at hipguide.com, a trend guide on cool places to go and what to wear, is one of the most accurate on-the-pulse fashion observers I know. She came up with this "date and time" reference system one day while we were sitting chattering away, waiting for a designer show to start at Fashion Week. It made so much sense to me, and it works every time, on every icon. (Although Syl would be the first to remind me that by definition icons and iconic moments are in the past, which means true icons are people who are already dead. Eek!) However, nailing down a fashion moment in time is a really neat way for you to break down the elements of iconic style and learn how to build them up for yourself.

Think of Audrey Hepburn's most iconic moments. Don't they all seem to happen in the 1960s at noon? Do you know what I mean? The Capris, the flats, the outdoorsy vibe, and so on. The whole look in which she was so frequently photographed fits perfectly with this era and time of day and it never wavers—a sure sign that she has real iconic status. Marilyn Monroe on the other hand, was different. She was always associated with night. She was never a daytime girl. We could argue that she was a real "dress person," as she was rarely seen in pants. Since Marilyn's dresses were always the most tightly fitted corseted looks, we could put her down as an 8 p.m. girl. But she's an 8 p.m. girl in the 1950s at the best supper club in town! Do you get my drift?

Now let's apply the system to a modern icon. Take Gwen Stefani. She's clearly picked the 1940s as her decade, but she's picked 1940s daytime, as she always wears red lipstick and always wears her hair in a pin curl or chignon, rarely down. Gwen marries this retro glam thing with a rock edge even when she's wearing her own label, a very cool and often Rastafarian-colored line of street clothing. So she's 1940s daytime Rastafarian! It sounds really weird, but this style is simply an expression to describe that she's a pretty darn happening icon that everyone watches very closely.

If you are not comfortable picking a decade, you could pick a place instead, say Paris, France, or Palm Beach, Florida. These two destinations evoke very different but clear style cues. Either way, when you are figuring out how to position yourself, pick two influences from a decade, date, time, and place, and you will anchor yourself with some iconic style.

Create a persona

Creating a persona is a way of living another fashion life as your alter ego. If you create a whole other *being* that screams your style, then this imaginary person functions as your internal fashion checklist. Whether you think of your-self as a trendsetter or a style icon, this alter ego can act as a filter. It's like having an internal personal stylist on hand to help you make fashion decisions every day. Unsuitable fash-ion pairings or selections are much more easily filtered out. Say your persona is "aloof upper-class art historian" or "aris-tocratic heiress." Before trying something on or making a purchase, you should ask yourself, would my alter ego, the aristocratic heiress, buy this pocketbook? Would it suit her style or keep with her personality? If the answer is no, then thankfully the persona functions as a great impulse-buying protection policy! But the main use is to keep your personal style consistent. It's how you see yourself, by modeling yourself on someone else.

One of the most common mistakes in fashion is that people directly try to copy by purchasing pieces seen on someone whose body type doesn't imitate their own. Gwyneth Paltrow sure wears beautiful long dresses on her willowy frame well, but if you're petite and flat-chested, you can't necessarily copy her look without looking out of pro-portion.

Claim a signature accessory

Liz Taylor's signature accessory is her jewelry, but not just any jewelry. Liz is known for her big gala Oscar-worthy jew-elry including big clusters of pearls, giant diamonds, and meteor-sized cocktail rings. So famous is her signature acces-sory that Liz even went into business making a line of jew-elry under her own name.

So, here is the tip: go ahead and claim a signature acces-sory. Pick something that you are drawn to, that you really love, and that others have complimented you on in the past. No matter what it is, you will need to stick with this as your theme regardless. It could be flats, it could be purple toe polish, and it could be lots and lots of bangles worn on your left arm. Whatever it is, it needs to suit you, flatter one of the best parts of your body, and mix in consistently with your look day in, day out. My eminently stylish cousin Lilian wore red Chanel nail polish that was never chipped, and this immaculate paint job beautifully showed off her elegant and expressive fingers. She wore some of the most flamboyant eveningwear and had an Imelda Marcos-sized collection of Chanel suits, but no matter what, her Chanel red nails were her signature. The expressive hands with the red nails accessorized with gold rings are her legacy, and always will be.

Strike a pose!

What separates the interesting and uniquely stylish from the ordinary can be something as simple as a walk, a pose, a stance, or other gesture beyond the clothing, which calls you out from the rest. In terms of a clotheshorse, it will be more about the way the clothes are worn, with a casual insouciance or an aristocratic air.

Style File

Don't let the clothes wear *you*—take charge and wear the clothes. It's the way you carry a look that really matters.

Some celebrities have managed to corner their "look" like this too. They know their good side or best stance and always hold the same pose when being photographed. If you can master the same thing for yourself in front of the mirror (without turning into a complete narcissist!), it is a way to find some extra inner confidence that helps you wear your clothes better. As far as posture goes, nothing looks worse on anyone, however well dressed, than walking or plodding along like a horse. Whatever you do, watch your posture. Hold your head up high and walk straight and purposefully. Or pick a look or attitude (maybe grunge or punk-rocker chic) that specifically suits your sloppy slouch! It will make a huge difference in how you are perceived. Think graceful or strong, aristocratic or serene, or whatever attitude exudes your persona. When you do this, you will instantly feel a lot more attractive—and confident! Remember, too, that even the most ordinary outfit can be made extraordinary by your hair, body language, posture, pose, and walk. These elements combine to create an overall great composition that exudes your personal vibe at any time. Think of it as your personal style ecosystem that has a balance all its own.

Create a vintage lifestyle

In trying to figure out clues for your iconic style, think further about your lifestyle choices. What music do you love, and what moods do you have? Are you a girl who always has a dirty Martini in hand? (You may be a Gary Grant era gal.) Or are you more of a clean-cut gin and tonic person, a throwback to the 1920s perhaps? Me, personally, I'm a milkshake kind of person, and the more chocolatey and the thicker the better! But there are clues to my signature or iconic style in this. I *do* actually love the classic 1950s diner blues and pinks. They make me happy. Call it coincidence, but I look good in these colors too. I'm very much a pink bubbly milkshake kind of girl. So watch your preferences and your style, and see if they don't coincide!

My HipGuide pal Syl's drink is champagne. It's just her drink. She orders it everywhere she goes. She's a quirky and cool dresser, and her lifestyle habits go with her fun fashion sense. So you can use your lifestyle habits to pick your clothes.

Are you stuck for clues or cues for your iconic style? Why not spend an afternoon watching a nice big batch of old movies? You'll get something from them even if it's just a big old case of nostalgia.

WHAT NOT TO CREATE

There are many, many pitfalls to beware of while trying to figure out your signature style, your signature item, or your reincarnation of yourself, if you are going to try it as a style icon.

Beware of any head-to-toe look

It serves no purpose if you've picked an era such as the 1960s, and you just don't add any modern twist to it at all. You'll just look like you are stuck in a retro time warp. That's both boring and potentially kind of scary! The same goes for copying piece by piece any one look you see on a celebrity. If you must be a dedicated celebrity style watcher, the key is to pick up just elements from other trendsetters and make them your own.

Beware of vintage eras that don't suit your body type

Please, please don't pick an era that clashes with your physical build. This sounds obvious, but 1960s was the era of Twiggy and skinny, skinny girls and miniskirts that worked on skinny legs. If you're a gym buff and are toned and muscular, the Twiggy look probably isn't the smartest choice for you. Try instead a more forgiving combination of iconic moments. The fifties nipped-in waist look is a great era for anyone whose waist is her best feature. But I'm not suggesting that you go out immediately and fill your closet with fifties day dresses, just that you keep in mind the style that flatters you the most and seek it out whenever possible. If you know you have fabulous thin ankles, maybe your style accessory is red-hot toes and strappy heels, no matter whether it's winter or summer.

Don't label yourself

One last thing, don't ever—whatever you do—*call* yourself a style icon or a trendsetter. These are monikers that others must bestow on you! You could call yourself "a dedicated follower of fashion" or "style obsessed," or you could leak your persona as something you aspire to. When someone compliments you on your gray sweater, you can say, "Oh thanks, it's from the part of me that channels my serious librarian!" or whatever else your persona may be. But remember, it's up to others to label you. It's really not cool to label yourself!

WHAT TO SHOP IN MAY

* Lightweight summer dresses
* Knit tops
* Lightweight tanks and tees

It's the perfect time to pick out *lightweight summer dresses* and maybe even a knit or two for wearing on top for those cooler days and nights. This month is also the time you should restock or replace all your *lightweight tanks and tees*.

All the racks will be brimming with fun and flirty spring

and summer dresses for day and night. To be able to get your size and favorite style in all the prints available, go shop for them now! Pull out a dress that worked for you in a past season. Is it a halter neck? Is it below the knee? Examine why it works on you. To save time keep that feature in mind when you go shopping for your dresses. Since it's early in the season and it may barely be warm enough to wear a dress, it's also a good time to think about how you can wear any new dress purchase through the fall to extend its life. Will the dress you choose be suitable to wear with boots? Would it be too long to wear with your favorite winter coat? Think about the long lifespan of a dress as they are such great wardrobe solutions and can go further than you think.

The other reason for buying the dress right now is that often it needs alterations. Especially if you come across a formal dress that you know you'll need for a specific event. We're not all the same size, shape, and proportion, and bringing up a hem a little or shortening a strap or two can make a huge difference even on a lower-priced dress, making it look more as if it was made for you. Do make the investment with either a tailor or your mom or grandma or a friend who can help if you don't feel you can make tailoring adjustments yourself. If you do all this now, when the time comes for wearing the dress, you won't drag it from the closet and remember that it's too long or too low and need to send it out right away, rendering it useless for another week.

Now, let's address the tanks and tees issues. You're going to have to do one of the hardest wardrobe purges of the year. The "T-shirt revival" I call it. It's the moment where all those seemingly okay white tees are going to hit the dust because you're going to replace each and every one of them. They may not look gray right now. But wait until you bring home just one shiny new white one, it'll make the old stock look like dishrags, and that's exactly what they should be used for. Funny enough, tanks are so much a part of our modern wardrobe, they've sort of become married as one into the family of jeans and denim. There are so many kinds of tanks and tees, some more expensive than others, but one thing is for sure, you need lots of them. I learned this from careful observation of my friend Caroline who owns a collection of very cool and fabulous New York boutiques called Pookie & Sebastian.

Caroline's my inspiration on tanks and tees not least because of the huge stock that flies out of her stores, but because as a true fashion insider she is someone who is always wearing pristine tanks. It's practically her uniform. So how many tanks should you get? Well, when Caroline's shipments come in, she literally takes out six white, six black, a few in camel, plus a few other colors that suit her; then she doubles up on her favorite color. So now I do the same, and I pass the information directly on to you. It's as simple as that. Thankfully, you don't need to own a clothing store to shop like this.

Tanks and tees are so affordable that everyone can have this kind of full-on tanks and tees wardrobe. Remember that tanks and tees are one of the least expensive items yet are one of the most versatile and accessible. I mean, what else can you wear from bed to the office and out after work with jeans? Reaching for a fresh tank or tee without needing to go near the laundry in the middle of summer is one of life's little affordable pleasures. Embrace it! If your bust size can be controlled by a tank with a built-in shelf bra, these are outstandingly useful and often overlooked, so don't forget to watch for these two-in-one miracles.

Layering tees, too, is a really good styling trick and a great way to get a different look from this basic item, so don't pass up unusual colors. Layering two colors that pick up the print in a skirt or pants that you pair with them can be really cool and make outfits more interesting. Beware though, you can't layer shelf-bra tanks, they don't fit on top of each other! Also, when you're buying your tees, just spare a thought for the bra you will need to wear underneath. Make a mental note of whether the racerback with a crossover or your good strapless bra would be best. The shapes you pick will depend on your body type. In general high crew shapes look preppy and conservative and work with trousers and as a classic look. Racerback tanks are the sexiest with strapless bras underneath and are particularly good for rounded shoulders. These are great to mix with a delicate skirt without trying too hard. Ballet style is casual off the shoulder and is alluring, feminine, and sporty all rolled into one. Adjustable straps make tanks really fit well. And baby doll styles look a little like lingerie if you are skinny and are flattering for early and late pregnancy. Lycra in tanks means they hold their shape better, so I think the perfect style is a Lycra cami with a built-in bra and adjustable straps. It can be worn under everything to give support and make your figure appear smooth or worn just by itself. However, remember that tanks with Lycra added will fit snugly to the body, and on a very hot summer day will not be as cool as those that are looser and made of 100 percent cotton. Be careful how you wash your most fabulous or expensive tees with glitter or crystals stuck on them. The most careful way to do this is to turn them inside out and wash them by hand or gently in the machine; then dry flat. They really last longer than the assault from getting washed with everything else.

TIPS FOR A LOWER TAB

If you decide that you want to evolve into a true style icon, you'll potentially save a ton of cash! This is because your choices will remain narrower for shopping since you will have claimed your "signature item" and your "look" and "era." As long as you take care when dressing each day to make style decisions that stay true to your chosen era or look, choosing your outfit will become easier and easier. Each day that you add your signature item, your vision of your style will become clearer and clearer until one day you'll know instinctively exactly what to wear. Getting dressed from that day forth will become completely automatic. The items you select for yourself will vary slightly seasonally, of course. You can either splurge or save on your signature piece, but you won't need items that don't fit within the framework of your look. Wonderfully, you're freed from the pressure of "buying in" to a trend that's hip and hot for the season but doesn't fit your new personal style. It's no wonder that terminally cool style icons look so confident. They have it so sorted out! There's no anxiety in what they wear or what to get dressed in. Their theme is so clear that even their less fashionable friends are able to predict what their own style icons would wear to an upcoming event.

If your budget is skinny this month but you want to try to replace your tanks and tees, look for a three-pack of plain white or black that are available in some pharmacies or discount stores like Wal-Mart or Kmart. They carry bulk package purchases like this that are supergood buys as long as you try one on first to see that the cut and fit suits you.

Tips for saving on buying dresses boils down to quality, not quantity. Just one or two new dresses that look great on you will do you well if you are on a supertight budget, especially if you choose styles that coordinate with sweaters and accessories from past seasons. This is especially true if you find a dress that is good for both day and night—a rare animal, indeed. If you can, choose dresses in silk or cotton and spandex mix. A lined dress with a good structure will last for ages too. A good dress need not be complicated or with much detail so long as you add treasured accessories like earrings, necklaces, shrugs, sweaters, boots, or shrunken cardigans—even belts change up the tempo and get different looks going. If you have a little more to spend, you may want to pick dresses that function for different times of the day: a day dress, a night dress, an all-purpose beachy dress, and an occasion dress. Make your choices very different, and you will be able to work them to death.

Don't get four dresses the same weight and length. Perhaps get a 100 percent cotton calf-length strapless dress for those lazy beach weekends, a chiffon floor-skimming halter party dress for summer cocktails, an A-line quirky-print rayon-mix dress doing double duty at work and after out on the town, and a classic black sleeveless knee-length sheath strictly for business. Perhaps you could jazz up your beach dress with accessories for an evening out? If you know you need a dress for a particular upcoming event like a wedding or baby shower, try to get that selected first. At least you'll relax knowing you have your outfit ahead of time. Later it'll be up to you to make the dress work in other ways. You never know, it may end up being your most flexible all-purpose number. You may even crop it after its official debut and give it a longer life as a short sleeveless one. Fashion recycling to the rescue once again!

✳ JUNE ✳

Be the Best-Dressed Wedding Guest

Okay, let's get right to it. This dilemma creeps up on you each year around Memorial Day—the moment the wedding season starts in earnest. From TV producers to magazine editors to viewers and readers all over the country, everyone wants tips on how to be the best-dressed wedding guest. And the most frequently asked question from my friends and family is, What do I wear to that upcoming wedding? It's an annual fashion dilemma that repeats itself each year, and unless you're in the wedding party or are actually the bride(!), there are many factors to consider and even etiquette to take into account. So let's break it down so that you'll never have to wonder again.

We all want to be able to pick out the perfect outfit each time we're invited to a wedding. Ultimately, when dressing for a wedding, you should have a feeling of total confidence, as if you could never be left off the best-dressed list ever or never wear the wrong combinations. Another goal for you is to be sure not to draw more attention to yourself than is polite, by upstaging the bride or wedding party, and *never* get dressed for a wedding in a vulgar way. All that said, wedding attire is a bit of a minefield because even good taste worn inappropriately will leave the same negative lasting impression as bad. The ideal is to dress appropriately while incorporating your own stylish flair. Receiving a wedding invitation shouldn't fill you with dread over what to wear, but instead with stylish inspiration.

Without your putting undue pressure on yourself, it pays to get it right when dressing for a wedding. Just remember that what you wear to a wedding is recorded in photographs and even on video these days. If you are close to the happy couple, your choice of outfit could well end up in photo frames displayed on their mantel for decades to come, so pick wisely!

Okay, where do you start? Maybe you've got a great suit or a fun dress or unworn separates lurking in the back of the closet along with the usual suspects you pull out each time you think about getting dressed for such an event. How do you know which of your outfits to select? Or how do you know which kind of outfit you should be looking for to buy new?

WHAT OUTFIT CHOICES DO YOU HAVE?

Reading between the lines

When you receive a wedding invitation, it is likely to be packed full of all kinds of information to give you fashion cues to get started. Granted, some wedding invites that involve multiple events, rehearsal dinners, and so on, can be something to decipher, but check on a few details and you will be on your way to choosing what you should wear or pack in the case of a destination wedding.

Checking for location, location, location

Look at the location of the party and nuptials. Everything you need to know (all the clues) are in the invite. Read it and think. Is it a beach wedding taking place at dusk? Is the wedding in a church with a seated lunch afterward? Think about the place and time of day and match your wardrobe accordingly. If you are in a dilemma, it's always safer to dress up rather than dress down. Showing up too formal or overdressed is a much less punishable offense than being underdressed. (This one you should go to the gallows for.) A wedding is a party for the celebration of love! So, dress up!

Being aware that timing is everything

Do the ceremony and celebrations start after 5 p.m.? If so, you get the green light to wear eveningwear to the entire event even if it is broad daylight outside at the start time. Is it a wedding on an afternoon weekday with a cocktail hour-style celebration? You can just about get away with dressed-up business casual, but a skirt suit or a dress is better than a pantsuit even if you have come from work. Is the wedding on the evening of July 4th or on New Year's Eve? There is no harm in wearing patriotic colors, something vaguely themed, but be subtle, very subtle.

Having an actual theme

Some brides request that everyone wear white, a uniform that is so easy and simple and looks gorgeous in photos. If so, the theme is actually written on the invite. It may read Dress: Vintage Victorian or Dress: Yankees. If you see this type of directive on a wedding invitation, you know you are in for a fun wedding, but keep in mind that you are attending a wedding, not a costume party. So have fun with your outfit while respecting the bride's wishes. If there is no actual theme but you need inspiration for something fresh and interesting to wear, think local. Is the wedding party venue near or beside the water? It might be appropriate to wear a nautical-inspired outfit. Or you can always pick out an accessory or wear a color or a piece of jewelry that complements the theme. Do not play this one too kitsch, but it can be great to have on an accessory that is a neat talking point with other guests.

Knowing if you have time for a quick change

Do you suspect that there might be time to change between the ceremony and the party? The cues will be in the invite. It might say something like ceremony at 6:00 p.m., cocktails and photos at 7:30 p.m. and dinner at 8:30 p.m. In other words, unless you are in the wedding party, the photographer will monopolize the wedding party for a good hour after the ceremony while the rest of the guests are treated to an extra long cocktail hour. If you know that the wedding and dinner are set up in the same hotel and you are in from out of town and staying there, you can easily keep your change of outfit ready upstairs and disappear briefly to primp up. If you change your clothes, you change the energy you put out. You give yourself a different high, and guests feeling this good make the occasion feel extra special. This is a great ploy if the wedding is formal or religious, but you know the bride and groom well and know that they want the celebration part of the evening to be a much wilder event!

Your dressing dilemma in this situation is resolved. You have no need to find an outfit that works for both the formality of the ceremony and the groovier tone of the party. Here you can pick a classic look for the "I do" part and a dancing dress for the "party all night" part. One note however: this is not a chance to outshine the bride or to skip out on a chunk of the party. If everyone did this, there would be no cocktail hour, so do it swiftly. This is more about a matter of convenience and changing the energy of the event. If anyone asks or comments on why you changed, just say you really wanted to dance later and went to get comfortable. It will loosen other people up.

Taking the religious hint

If the invite refers to part of the ceremony taking place in a house of worship or another religious arena or somewhere abroad that is really exotic, bear in mind that it may be respectful both for men and women to be covered up in some way. If you sense that the nuptials have a deeply religious tone, call the bride or another guest to confirm proper dress. If you don't know anyone close to the bride, you can always call the house of worship or temple listed on the invite (so read it carefully) and ask an administrative person what the expected dress code is for the religion, temple, or house of worship.

WHAT TO WEAR WHERE

How do you figure out what to wear where? With many more nuptials erring on the side of informal and trending toward unconventional ceremonies in unusual locales, think about how you see yourself working the party. Will you be sitting for most of the time? If so, you won't want to pick something restrictive. Are you likely to eat with a plate balanced on your lap or while standing? If so, extraneous accessories like shawls or hats could be cumbersome and irritating. Then there are other factors to keep in mind too—like appropriate footwear if the event is outside and the time and temperature of the day. Here are some guided examples to help you plan.

A *beach wedding*

If the wedding is on the beach, you should immediately know that the focus of your outfit for the event will not be shoes! But if you are not sure, ask the bride or, again, call the venue on the invite and or someone else close to the bride who should know the format of the wedding. Just because the wedding is on the beach does not mean it will be completely casual. There are levels of beach wedding formality. The kind of wedding that has all the guests just standing casually on a bluff is not the same as one that has chairs and a

Style File: Casualties of Casual Dressing

Think about the length of your dress. It may work well with killer shoes, but at a barefoot event, the length could drop to an unflattering level.

walkway to reach them without actually touching the sand. For this type of wedding, shoes will count!

In general, beach destination weddings call for a resort-style flowing sundress, either strapless or halter neck or short sleeved or cap sleeved, but not cotton jersey, the kind that you wear to the beach on an average day. Look for or scour your closet for something that moves with the breeze. Chiffon is always a fun choice. A silk blend is great, too, as are silk separates or a 100 percent silk dress paired with a slip underneath if sunlight might pass right through it! Be careful not to pick something that you know is too hot to wear as you will want to stay cool. Beware that linen and some cotton and linen mix fabrics will crease terribly and won't travel well to the beach even in a garment bag. These are a good choice in theory, but in practice, you risk the wrinkle factor. You can always try hanging the linen dress in the hotel bathroom and filling the room with steam from a hot shower if you're heading to a beach destination wedding, but if this fails, be prepared to iron on-site.

If you're über stylish or worried about too much sun, you might get away with a tight-fitting sunhat or straw trilby, but that's optional if you decide once at the location that it's really too windy and could blow away. If the wedding is at dusk with the reception running into the night, you won't need a hat, but then a gorgeous shawl or shrug in an accent color will save you from both the cold and sand flies after dark. As for accessories, keep them a light color for an overall effect of lightness and, in general, less formal. A flowy chiffon dress does not demand a city-style structured pocketbook to go with it! An embellished straw bag or an unstructured bag like a fabric clutch is likely to be more suitable on the beach. Scour your closet before you go to make sure you pair some destination-appropriate accessories with your choice of outfit.

A *city hotel or banqueting hall with a seated lunch celebration*

Okay, there are three huge clues here: The wedding is in a hotel or banqueting hall, it's during the daytime, and it's a seated event. Clearly, you don't need to dig out your dancing dress. This is a civilized get-together, and likely to be very chic. Think elegance here, but also think decorous. No flapping bingo wings (flabby upper arms) poking out of shift dresses; pick something more forgiving like kimono sleeves or long skinny embellished cardigans over sexy day dresses. Pretty pared-down unique separates (not necessarily tailored—those days of structured suits and their expected formality are gone) with a hat would be perfect. A skirt suit with a hat if you have one is just as chic but not as fashion forward, just a slightly more conservative option. PS: It's okay to eat lunch in your hat, there's no need to remove it!

> **NB**: According to *Emily Post's Etiquette* (New York: Funk & Wagnalls, 1923): "Details of Etiquette at Luncheons. . . . Fashionable ladies *never* take off their hats." Weddings are no different. So if you wear a hat, you can keep it on! While pantsuits are perfectly acceptable, they are not as good a choice as skirts or dresses for a wedding, which are dressier and more ladylike no matter the weather or the season. But if you only wear pantsuits in life, just make sure you choose one that is nicely cut. Long skirts or three-quarter length embellished skirts paired with high sandals or boots (depending on the weather) are perfectly fine options for a wedding brunch or lunch. With this type of event, you might already have a dressy enough outfit from your current separates without going out to buy anything new.

An informal outdoor or country wedding followed by a casual buffet-style party

The clues here are outdoor, country, and buffet. Immediately, you should think of standing on turf. How good would spike heels be? Remind yourself that this can sometimes be ridiculous. A tasteful pair of flats is fine for a casual, outdoorsy wedding party with a buffet. If the country wedding is happening in a specially erected tent, then you can figure in that there is likely to be a walkway, a structure, and even a dance floor. So find out. Also for outdoor weddings or country weddings, plan your look for later in the evening for when it gets chilly. Select a contrasting wrap or another interesting layer that does not detract from the sexiness or mood of your dress or separates. A floral party dress or a silk top or shell and skirt are usually the right combination for country-casual weddings. Suits can be too constricting and too uptight looking for this type of occasion. Really smart wedding guests who attend many country weddings and wear summer dresses even squirt some bug spray on their legs and feet before they leave the house just to guard against pests. It is most unladylike to be scratching and bending and swatting throughout any part of the ceremony or party.

WEDDING GUEST DRESS
ETIQUETTE Q&A

Everything you ever wanted to know about wedding wardrobe etiquette, but were afraid to ask!

Q: Can I wear black?

A: Well, yes and no. It sure is chic and perfect for after-six events in cities, but it shouldn't be your first choice. Black is a somber and serious color, and weddings are fun and joyous. My rule is that if the wedding is in a metropolitan city in the wintertime and the party is after six or after dark, then yes, go ahead, wear black, but only if you really can't find anything else that works. If you feel super safe in black, you could try a dress in chocolate brown or navy blue. These are very chic colors, and have the same slimming and confidence-building effects as black without looking like you are at a funeral party.

Q: Can I wear black if I'm pregnant?

A: If you're pregnant and feel really big, you go ahead mom-to-be; anything black is a go. Be sure though to accessorize large like your belly is. Nothing looks sillier than itsy-bitsy jewelry on big momma! Think about the possibilities of a large necklace or large statement earrings to dress up the black. This keeps the focus away from the belly bulge and near the glowing face!

Q: What size handbag should I carry?

A: Pick the smallest pocketbook you can for a wedding. It's just chicer. And you don't need to take your life to the party. Be the life of the party instead. This is like your personal Oscars. No one carries a big old bag down that red carpet. If you've ever closely watched a red-carpet event, you'll see that in fact, lots of movie stars don't carry a pocketbook at all. Their dates or publicists who trail a foot behind sometimes keep their keys and lipstick safe or hold their very small pocketbooks for them. The effect is that of a glamorous woman who looks *so* unencumbered. But if you must, just a small one with barely room for the necessities of keys, money, a lipstick, and cell phone will do.

Q: Is it ever appropriate to wear white to a wedding?

A: Unless the bride specifically requests it, as mentioned earlier, don't wear white. Don't wear a white dress or even off-white or even an off-white pantsuit. It's not poor etiquette exactly, but later, in group photos, you'll draw attention away from the bride (if she's in white or cream). Wearing white to another person's wedding really is one of those queer fashion things, not quite a rule, more a "dare you not" sort of thing. Even if you're a statement dresser and normally like to stand out, you may end up feeling a bit embarrassed if other people comment that you're wearing white and are competing with the bride.

Q: Should I wear heels to a beach wedding?

A: No. If the wedding is on the sand and if you must bring heels for wearing later, kick them off and go barefoot for the ceremony. You can dance all night in them afterward.

Q: What should my date wear?

A: Keep your date in check! No matter how formal or casual the occasion, your date should be dressed appropriately. For example, don't ever let him wear shorts to a beach wedding. Set the standard for decorum with proper, tasteful dressing. He may not need a tie or a jacket for an informal destination beach party, but keep those legs of his covered. Unless the wedding is in Bermuda. I'm not joking! This is really the only place on planet Earth your man can wear shorts to a wedding, and they better be Bermuda-length shorts! You set the tone and make him dress in line with you.

Also, beware not to clash your colors as you are likely to be photographed together. Just a piece of an accent color from his tie could be the mainstay of your dress, or have the red trim on his shirt pick out the flower details on your hat. Be subtle, but coordinate with each other, and if possible, make sure you know what he is wearing beforehand. Beware, too, that some men are shop-a-holics. They arrive at a destination wedding a day or two before the ceremony and feel very much as if they are on vacation. For them that means a big fast shopping trip. Just make sure he knows what you have planned to wear to the party before he comes back from the outlets with lots of new ideas for himself that do not coordinate with you at all.

While we are on the subject, be sure to dress at the same level of formality too. If you are in a full-length gown, the full Oscar getup, it can look odd if he is not wearing a tie or his suit is super casual. You set the tone, you be the lead fashionista as a couple, and you do the planning.

Q: *Can I wear my sunglasses in wedding photos?*

A: No. It doesn't matter if you're at a casual outdoor beach affair or posing with the bride on the steps of a city church, always remove your sunglasses for the photos. Please. Pretty please! No excuses on this one. No one should look like the secret service or the mafia in someone's happy nuptial photos or at the party afterward.

Q: *What should I do with my pocketbook during the reception?*

A: When the dancing and partying portion of the evening is in full swing, it's really tempting to leave your pocketbook, especially if it's a very small pocketbook, on the table. But don't. Place it in your lap when at the table or under your chair instead. Although this is more of a small behavior etiquette than a true fashion "don't," it's something that feels to me to be tightly linked to your overall appearance, so why spoil the image?

FASHION-FORWARD PLANNING

No matter what the venue, here are a few things you should do before attending any type of wedding event.

Get thee to the dry cleaners

Make sure your chosen outfit cleaned, ironed, steamed, pressed, and infused with the smell of roses or whatever else you have to do to it a good week in advance of the event. There's nothing worse than finding a stain or crease on your otherwise perfect outfit on the day of a wedding or big celebration. Think ahead, and always have an alternative outfit on standby in case of an emergency or a sudden change of plans or unexpected weather change.

Get your underthings ready

If you're planning on wearing hosiery or a shaper or falsies or stick-ons under a dress to make it fit better or make it more decent, get out and buy them ahead of time (two pairs for insurance!). Nothing like the stress of scrabbling in the underwear drawer for the right strapless bra, untorn hose, or other imperfect underpinnings to start the day of nuptial celebrations off the wrong way.

Get your jewelry and accessories ready

Consider what jewelry you'd like to wear to the event and make sure you dig it out. Can you remember where you put it last? Just try it on to make sure it's not broken. Backstage at fashion shows, the dressers place their models' outfits and exact pieces of jewelry together all laid out perfectly so that they simply slip out of the old outfits and into the new ones. Sometimes the changes are so quick that models are literally running to make it back onto the runway. Your dressing should not be so hurried, but if you can borrow just one page from the pros when getting ready for a big party, be sure to plan your outfit and try it on ahead of time so that on the big day you can get ready without being in a rush.

Get thee to the cobbler

Make sure your favorite Manolos, Maddens, Choos, Zanottis, Kenneth Coles, or other *pied-à-wear* are in good repair. Visit the cobbler the week before the event for new soles or heel tips, if necessary. A wedding with dancing? This could end up a shoe emergency if you don't check your shoes beforehand, making sure the heels and tips are well in place. Also, if you've purchased new shoes, wear them out on the street for a few yards and deliberately scratch them up so that you won't slip on your backside on a shiny, slippery dancefloor as you make your John Travolta moves after too much champagne.

WHAT TO SHOP IN JUNE

* Dresses (if you have a hole in your collection)
* Skimpy tanks

June is a time to take it slow on the shopping front. You will need to save your money for big ticket purchases later in the year, so if you can control your spending and feel you have enough options for the warm weather, save this month's budget until the fall, as you will need it, trust me!

If the weather is unreasonably hot and you have funds to spare, add one or two extra pieces from the categories that you own, such as *dresses* or *tanks,* from the skimpier cooler versions that are in the stores now. Everything new now is likely to have spaghetti straps or require that you show a lot of skin. These pieces are usually lightweight versions of everything you already have, and that means you don't have to buy them. Pick out one small thing so that you feel spoiled if you like, but save your spending for the big stuff that's coming down the line. If you must buy something, try bright or fashion-forward colors for a little fun. If you must hit the mall for some cooling therapy, go see for yourself that there isn't anything really new. A lot of stores hold mini-sales around the end of June, which goes to show that summer merchandise is getting old.

TIPS FOR A LOWER TAB

Finding a special outfit for a wedding is a challenge on a budget. However, accessories can totally transform a tired dress into something that really works great for an event.

Say you are a trendsetter and the trend right now is all about large pendant necklaces. Why not try your long sundress from a couple of seasons ago with the new trendy pendant you have and some contrasting fabulously stacked high heels from the present season? Just try it on all together and experiment. If it works, you will have saved tons of cash and time agonizing over what to wear, not to mention that mixing and matching things that you already have often yields a bonus outfit you never even thought of before.

Alternatively, you can drag out that formal bridesmaid's dress that you've been hiding in the back of your closet and change it up so it's cool and new to you again. Always a bridesmaid doesn't mean never being a best-dressed wedding guest! The bonus of altering a former dress that was made for you is that no one will recognize it, and this can be a refreshingly good excuse to attack something that was barely worn. If you can't see how to alter a former bridesmaid's dress to make it fun, modern, sexy, or alluring, take it to your tailor for inspiration. You can always decide not to do it if the cost sounds prohibitive or objectively you don't like yourself in the color after all.

If you're set on getting something new for a wedding, it could be new to you but not necessarily new. Designer consignment stores often have once-worn dresses or suits or other fancy wear that is over for a previous shopper but new to you and your wardrobe. For one third of designer prices, you could be lucky and pick up an outfit that is exactly your size and doesn't even need altering. Try hitting consignment stores in well-to-do neighborhoods as the offerings are likely to be more luxurious there.

* JULY *

The Jet-Set Wet Set

Wahoo! It's vacation time. Hopefully, you have some kind of neat summer break planned this month, even if it's just a short time-out over the fourth of July weekend. Nonetheless, if you're going away now or sometime in the future, the principles of packing and selecting your vacation wardrobe are the same. The idea is to edit your vacation wardrobe choices well in advance, selecting so carefully that eventually what you place in your bag is a *genius* capsule collection that'll make you feel totally secure and blown away when you open your case at your destination.

WHAT TO PACK AND WHAT NOT TO PACK, THAT IS THE QUESTION

Pack light!

You need to travel light. You need to pack light. You *can* pack light. You *can* travel light. If this sounds like the mantras and affirmations of a former pack-o-holic, you'd be right! And now for a slice of brutal honesty. Believe me, this hurts to say, but even though I've accumulated much fashion travel savvy over the years, sometimes I just *can't* pack light. I blame it on general travel anxiety and fear of leaving home(!) and not on a mutant style gene, but hey I'm only human. So if you're like I am, due to whatever hang-up, and you've packed your case, groaned under its weight, and unpacked it with the intention of editing heavily only to repack it with the same items, you have my sympathies. But packing light can be done whether or not you're traveling for business or pleasure. As I'm a recovering pack-o-holic, I pack beautifully light about three out of five trips. So, there you have it. It's okay if overpacking gets the better of you from time to time. This usually happens when you're going somewhere you've never been before.

If you're truly looking for a get-out-of-jail-free card on this, here are three excuses *not* to pack light:

1. The big ski trip is a trip that is nearly impossible to pack light for. Everything you need for this trip is very bulky, so knock yourself out and fill two cases or fill three if you do not mind paying the excess baggage fee. Better still, ship your stuff by FedEx or UPS ahead of time to your destination. This way there is no chance of an airline losing your luggage and you not hitting the slopes with all your swanky stuff. However, if you are making a really short trip and must bring only carry-on bags, the best tip is to wear your ski jacket and après boots to travel in to free up space.

2. An extended trip of two weeks or more especially if the season is wintry, is a definite overpack.

3. A Fashion Week attendance, be it Paris, London, New York, Milan, Tokyo, Moscow, LA, or anywhere else, gives you the green light *not* to pack light. Sound vaguely irrelevant? But it's that "what if" situation, and I wanted to cover all bases. If you're not in the fashion

Five Good Reasons to Pack Light

To aid you in your pack-o-holic recovery, I have come up with a list to help keep you on track:

1. You have freedom! If you can carry on your bag instead of checking it, this will make you more flexible with re-routing or other unexpected delights. Look at it this way: if you are stranded somewhere at least you will have all your stuff with you.

2. You can roll your own case without incurring a slipped disc.

3. You will have simple and pre-planned wardrobe choices, which creates more time for you to enjoy your trip.

4. You will have space in your bag to bring home new fabulous fashion finds should you see them on your travels.

5. You will have less laundry and dry cleaning on your return.

industry and you do find yourself invited to a Fashion Week event, you should know what it's like at one of these "insider conventions" (which is what they really are). You'll find them crawling with fashion editors, buyers, socialites, TV personalities, celebrities on the A-, B-, and C-list, tastemakers, stylists, and hangers-on of every fashion kind.

Some of these people will turn heaven and earth upside down to change outfits up to seven times a day, taking up residence in hotel suites and limousines to house their wardrobes while they navigate the schedule. Others will simply look chic from dusk to dawn in essentially the same outfit plus or minus a piece for variety. Having your own full-on arsenal of clothes handy for multiple different events on the same days and nights spent mingling among these same people will be a confidence booster even if you don't use your entire resources. Fashion Week is a totally unique fashion situation and a peculiar unreal slice of life.

But this gathering of the most highly critical fashion watchers whose lenses are on permanent zoom can teach us a few tricks for looking great to take back to the real world with us. (Changing outfits between wedding ceremony and after party at a hotel in the previous chapter is lifted straight from my experience at the shows.) That's not to say there isn't a downside. Sometimes the superconfidence, svelte figures, and attitudes of the fashion "editor" crowd can make an ordinary stylish person (without the larger-than-life ego) feel inadequate. Similarly, being around some of the most crucially hip and avant-garde dressers can make even a trendy dresser feel boring. Perhaps the best upside is that being around a group of people who push the envelope may encourage you to wear your most daring looks with confidence in future.

The bottom line is that even if you don't ever get to a fashion convention, the point is clear. If you have your own scary, overwhelming event at which you feel your style may be scrutinized even if you don't vary your outfits that much, simply having lots of choices while you're on the road will make you feel good. So give yourself wiggle room and not pack light if you're facing an extended weekend or week-long trip with multiple social reunions to get dressed for.

THE VACATION EDIT

Okay, so you're heading off for a summer getaway. It may sound a little dorky, but you might want to try to start packing a few days ahead of time. That way, at least subconsciously, you'll be mulling over not only what pieces you have but also what pieces you currently favor to take to your destination. Really, there's nothing dorky about preparation. Don't be surprised to find yourself making "aha!" breakthrough decisions about the items you'd like to pack while you're in the shower or fighting traffic during your weekday commute. When done right, packing is the sort of activity to mull over—it shouldn't ever be a split-second decision. Once the time comes to pack for a beach vacation, all sorts of fashion conundrums quietly emerge that are quite separate from the bathing suit anxiety, which thankfully you solved earlier in the year. Aren't you happy you did?

A *week before*

Here is what to do the week before your trip: Clear your bed if you haven't done so already as you will need to *see everything at once* for full preparedness packing. I do this when I'm packing for a TV segment in which I will be commentating on live TV in a city away from home. It is the only way to see your outfits and see what's missing.

On the left side of the bed, lay out your bathing suit choices, sarongs, or coverups and make a selection from your favorite summer footwear. While selecting shoes, remember the beach (think thongs), visualize activities you may take part in (need sneakers?), and think hard about heels. Are heels really wearable where you are going? Next, again to the left, lay out the dresses that you have in mind and the cardigans or sweaters: then lay out the selection of tees, tanks, and shorts. Last, find your toiletries bag and set it to one side.

Now, pick one outfit from the entire selection that you really know you will wear at the destination and yet would be comfortable traveling in, including the shoes. Remove it from the pile and lay it on the right-hand side of the bed. This stuff is going with you, except it's going *on* you. What you travel *in* should earn its keep, and it will. Pick something that recovers if creased or that rinses easily by hand if a spillage occurs. If the outfit is sleeveless, pick a contrasting or similar sweater or light jacket to keep warm on the plane or inside where the air-conditioning might be blasting or for cool evenings.

Next, pick an A-Team of bathing suits carefully, making sure you include ones that get wet, ones that stay dry, and one that is recycled, perhaps for a dunk in a super chlorinated Jacuzzi. Put these to the right-hand side of the bed separately. Then pick a B-Team selection. If there is room at the end of the edit, they will go, too, as they take up so little space. Europeans often have one bathing suit for each day of their trip, so if you really have a collection and are economical on the rest of your packing, why not take them all?

After that, pick the sarongs, pareos, long silk pants, or oversized shirts you plan to wear to take cover from the sun and also set them over on the right-hand side of the bed. Can't decide which wraps for which suits? Pick contrasting but complementary colors to your suits. If you're still having a problem deciding what goes with what, think about the signature colors of the most famous and swanky stores and take your cues from them. Got a brown suit? Bring your orange cover-up, and you'll strut around feeling very Hermès. Got a white suit? Pick out an aquamarine or duck egg blue shirt, and you have the classic Tiffany colors.

At least you know these color combos go great! If you've got a very colorful suit, bring along a neutral wrap. Tan, white, black, or navy are very smart. If your suits are plainer, hopefully, you've shopped colors to match them like pink or prints. Sunglasses can quite dramatically change the look of your suits and sarongs, so choose carefully from your fabulous stable of shades. Get your glamour suits matched with your metallic oversized aviators or your ethnic suits with your tortoiseshell shades. Match up your own combinations and lay them to the right.

So now that you have choices, your blueprint begins. Pick out one or two selections of daywear and one or two for evening. Lay them over on the right now too. How many ways can the items on the right be paired together? Would the bikini top from your get-wet bathing suit go with a skirt? Do your sunglass and sandal pairings create enough options for you? Could the cover-up in blue work as a shawl with the dress? Think about everything performing double duty, and adjust accordingly. Perhaps you prefer to substitute an item from the left for one on the right for more maximum use. Would it help if you re-select sandal choices that go better with the evening clothes and not just your bathing suits? Now, once you have your most solid choices picked out, leave the room!

Go do something else for a while and forget about your packing. While you're away from it, is there something niggling at you? A gut feeling? Something you really *want* to pack that's not in the pile to the right? Are you torn over the footwear? Do you really need sneakers? When you're ready, go back in and take another look at your choices. Be ruthless. Make new substitutions in order to aim for some variety. Does your traveling outfit still make sense, or is it too similar to something else on the right side of the bed now? Make everything work hard for its place in the case. Do you love every piece on the right, and can you see more than one way to wear it? Don't you dare pack your suitcase until you can.

Next, put everything on the left away in your closet. That's right, get it out of your sight so you don't have second thoughts. You're now left with your pure capsule travel collection. Then, pull out the correct underwear for the pieces you selected and stash them in a lingerie bag. Finally, select a few small but hard-working pieces of jewelry and place them in a jewelry wrap. Take stock of everything you've packed. Is there something missing? Is it something that you really, really need? Now you have time to go get it. Maybe that cute sundress could use a dry cleaning. Take it in; there's time. Maybe your favorite flip-flops aren't going to last another season. No need to panic; you still have time to pick up a new pair. That's another plus to this exercise—it gives you time to cover all your bases.

At this point you can store in your suitcase the shoes, swimwear, sunglasses, and other foldable items until the day before your trip. Hang up the dresses or other crease-worthy choices at the end of your closet rail until the day before you leave. This way you won't wear, make dirty, ruin, or damage any of the items you plan to pack.

The day before

Don't forget to retrieve the hanging choices from your closet; then starting with the shoes first, you can now begin to pack your bag. The stress of what to bring expired a week ago, didn't it? It lightened up your load for the trip. Good job.

STAYING CHIC IN THE SHADE

Okay, you don't want skin cancer or heat rash or sunburn on your vacation, but you do want to look and feel cool. So at some point or another, you will need a cover-up from the heat. Be it a sarong, pareo, long chiffon pants, or shirt, something chic for the shade should accompany your bathing suits in your case. Sunhats and sunglasses are a given and are as important to maintaining and protecting hair color and vision as they are to looking cool. My personal favorite for any warm-weather trip, however, is the sarong. They take up very little room, they look fine even when creased or wrinkled, and they can be used in many different ways. However versatile it is, a sarong is a cover-up. However you wear it (except as a shawl), it should be worn in conjunction with a bathing suit.

Here are my six top ways to use a sarong:

1. **As a miniskirt modesty wrap**: Fold in half longways and wrap around your waist. Where the fabric meets on itself, tuck in or roll over to secure. It should stay in place if you tuck it tightly. Great for eating lunch while still in your bikini beach style but with some consideration for decorum!

2. **As a head turban**: This works only if your sarong is small and made of very lightweight cotton weave. Fold your sarong so that it measures approximately 20 inches by 36 inches. Then throw your hair forward as if you are toweling it dry, and use the sarong as you would a towel to hold all your hair. Now twist it as you bring your head up and tuck the ends under at the nape of your neck. This look is great for protecting hair and hair color from the sun, but it can also get a bit hot, so it's a style best utilized while hair and or sarong are wet!

3. **As a strapless dress:** Wrap the sarong around your back and hold the two ends in front of you by your bust as high as you can with the top of the sarong under your armpits. Either tie the ends in a large knot in front of your bust or neatly tuck in the ends under the armpits. If you have a skinny belt, this can look great added to accentuate your waist.

4. **As a halter dress:** Stand with the sarong around your back as before with the ends out in front of you, and pulling the fabric taut, pull each end over the opposite shoulder and tie in a loose knot at the back of your neck. Adjust the cowl neck part in the front to flatter your bust and bathing suit line. This rather loose, roomy cowl neck halter dress is quite cool to wear and great for a walk down the beach.

5. **As a towel:** You can keep the sand off and dry off just as well with a sarong as with a bulky beach towel. You may have to anchor it with stones or shoes as the thin material will flap in the sea breeze, but it will dry more quickly as it's so thin. This is perfect for occasions when you want to skip carrying a bulky towel or for a last beach visit (once you've packed to return home) before you leave, since a damp sarong will fit in a ziplock bag to take home.

6. **As a shawl or bug protector:** Fold the sarong in half longways and simply use it as you would a pashmina or shawl around your shoulders. If the bugs are biting your ankles at an outdoor dinner, remove it from your shoulders and tuck it as a discreet blanket over your legs to stop the massacre! If you are out really late and the evening cools, just this one layer of cotton will suffice as a warmer blanket worn as a scarf, as a shawl, or as a blanket on the legs.

Sarong Style

If you are really handy at the sewing machine or have a good tailor, here is an incredibly easy modification you can do to your sarong to make it always simple to wear (or this is how to make your own perfectly fitting sarong from scratch). PS: This works best with the slinkier sarongs made with some rayon.

1. Take the sarong and lay it out across a table with access to the long side.

2. Place a cereal bowl upside down on the top right-hand corner of the fabric and trace a line around the outside of the bowl with tailor's chalk where the bowl hits the fabric. Cut out this fabric.

3. Do the same with the top left-hand corner of the fabric.

4. Sew some binding or braiding material (something that coordinates with the sarong's colors) around the cut edge of the fabric where the cereal bowl outline is. This will nicely finish off what are now armholes.

5. Do the same with the left side.

6. Put it on by holding the sarong out in front of you. Place your right arm through the new left armhole loop. Then, wrapping the rest of the sarong fabric across your body, passing it behind you, place your other arm in the right loop. Voila! A dress-slash-sarong that stays on.

The beach emergency kit

We can't talk about going to the beach without a mention of how this fine example of a location-specific kit really comes into its own. As far as its contents go, there are a few essentials that any kit should have, but only you know what your hair does at the beach. Likewise, you're the best judge of your skin protection. So only you know what your personal essentials are for a great beach emergency kit. A small but effectively stuffed one can be blissful at the beach.

My personal picks for the perfect beach emergency kit

Start with a clear ziplock bag or large cosmetic purse and pull together the following:

* *A spare bikini stashed inside a smaller ziplock bag:* (A fast neat trick of the socialite set who bounce from private yacht to private yacht! They swim in the ocean with their airtight ziplock bags tightly in hand, and miraculously at their new destination after a quick restroom visit, they emerge in a dry suit.) You can just as easily slip into the restroom or do a miracle strip under a sarong and change yours. Perhaps to eat lunch or get into the car to drive home? Either way you have a new style option.

* *Sunblock for the face and body:* It should be fresh, new sunblock that you bought recently. This stuff does expire, and so you must replace your stash in good time. Don't carry leftovers forward from one year to the next.

* *Small refillable spritzer bottle filled with tap or bottled water:* You can chill this overnight in the fridge if you like, and if you're hanging out with someone who carries a cooler of cold drinks, sneak it in there to keep it cold! It's for a quick spray of the face just to refresh or wash off the salty ocean. It also works great for spritzing sticky hands.

❋ *Lip balm or lipstick with SPF housed in a tiny lipstick case with a mirror inside:* The case insulates the lippy, keeping if from getting too melty. The mirror is handy for even sunscreen application and other discreet checks.

❋ *Hairbands and barrettes:* Pin up your hair when necessary.

❋ Baby wipes in a resealable packet. Use to clean hands before eating and to prepare for touching your face to adjust your beach beauty touches.

❋ *Money, money, money:* Even if you are going to hang out at a friend's pool, someone may offer to make a trip to the store for snacks, and you'll have the cash right there in your beach emergency kit sitting in your bag. You won't have to move a muscle. In a public beach setting, you could need it for parking, umbrella rentals, or buying yummy things like ice cream or coconuts (in really exotic places!). You won't even have to get up off your towel or out from under your umbrella if you keep a little extra cash in your beach bag.

❋ *A soft hat:* A baseball cap in a light color that you never wear at home will do in a pinch in your kit to give you extra sun protection or to keep glare off you if you take a dip. It's also good if you get asked to play an unexpected game of water polo or volleyball. A regular sunhat (which you might already have in your beach bag) won't do for this.

❋ *A pair of lightweight, dangling, inexpensive beachy earrings:* Great for glamming up your suit if there is a scene at the beach or a pool-to-bar situation at hand!

* *A small comb:* Perfect for tidying slicked back hair after being in the water.

* *A waterproof mascara for foolproof outdoor primping:* Maybelline's Great Lash is the world's best-selling one, and there's a reason—it stays on!

* *A tampon and a pad:* Always pack these for unexpected very unfashionable emergencies.

* *A small pouch of Kleenex tissues:* If you swim in the sea, the salt may drive you to clear your sinuses! And they are invaluable for wiping off anything from seagull gunk to gobs of spilt sunscreen.

* *A crossword puzzle:* This is a really cute thing to add that takes up no space because it's ripped out of a newspaper or magazine. Add a pen with a lid. It's a great relaxing conversation starter for a group and is the most lightweight entertainment you can pack.

Of course, you can personalize your kit with hair products that you can't live without or with an extra pair of contact lenses if you lose them when you swim! It's all up to you.

Beach-to-bar beauty

Heading straight from beach to bar without getting some downtime is a skill that can be learned. It's *so* cool to be able to do this. You can actually go eat a fancy meal in a restaurant right off the beach without ever returning to your room for excessive primping (with the right planning, that is). What I'm talking about is tweaking yourself so that you benefit from the extra boost in prettiness and confidence.

Here's how to do it and all while still sitting on your beach towel:

1. Take out your kit and add jewelry by way of earrings and a necklace, and you can even put on your watch. You feel dressed already, right?

2. Spritz your face with your fresh water and pat dry with Kleenex.

3. Slick your hair up or let it down, whichever is a change from the daytime version of you. If you have a hair product in your beach emergency kit, use it. Either wear your sunglasses on the top of your head as the sun goes down or pack them away.

4. Clean off your hands with a baby wipe. Apply fresh lipstick or lip balm and a fresh coat of your waterproof mascara.

5. Create a sexy but decorous outfit from the pieces of tops and bottoms that comprise your bikinis, your sarong, and the clothing you arrived in at the beach. Perhaps the top of the tankini that remained dry in the ziplock will work with the shorts you wore earlier in the day. Maybe instead it can be worn as a sexy halter top with your sarong as a miniskirt. Or perhaps your white shirt that acted as a cover-up can be tied sexily at the waist in a knot. Neatly roll up the sleeves to above the elbow to finish the beachcomber look. In a pinch you can take the belt from your shorts and cinch at the waist the strapless dress you made from your sarong.

6. Plan to take your jeweled thongs or fancier flip-flops before you leave home if you have the slightest inclination that you may get into a beach-to-bar situation (hey, there's room for spontaneity in life isn't there?). Hopefully, you are already wearing one or the other, and the look is now complete. Last, fold your beach

tote over the top and hold it like a clutch to look less cumbersome or carry it under your arm.

Practical après-sun fashion

Okay, you tried to stay cool, tried to stay out of the sun, and applied the mosquito repellent, yet somehow the downsides of summer still got the better of you and you're a sunburned, bug-bitten mess. Doesn't mean you have to look like one. With some practical help, you can prevent things from getting worse. If you weren't expecting mosquitoes or bugs but are inundated, reach for your long-sleeved coverup shirt to wear after dusk and pair that with palazzo-style or loose pants. If you're going for a moonlit walk on the beach, the sand flies may get the better of you if you don't cover your legs. If you're sunburned, loads of aloe and lotion will help to cool but also loose clothing will protect the skin from becoming more damaged. I'd say lose the bra if your top half is burned, since brassiere wires or restrictive elastic is a horrible companion for sunburned skin.

Channel your inner hippy with the sarong dress, long pants, a long loose dress, or a tunic look for a sunburn situation. Stick to all white for the coolest and most sophisticated look. Your silhouette may not be as figure hugging in an effort to be kind to your poor body, but you can add solid chunky jewelry to dress up floaty cotton clothes; it makes them look sophisticated. You'll know you've planned your packing right when, in this situation, you'll have the pieces to comfort yourself and still feel good. Better still, pack them in the first place. Loose clothes look just as chic as fitted pieces in hot weather—if not more so. Bon voyage!

WHAT TO SHOP IN JULY

* Long-sleeved tees
* Denims
* Lightweight sweaters

July is the time when stores hold sales. All the spring and summer preview stuff needs to be cleared out in preparation for the back-to-school onslaught that'll fill the shelves in August. Hopefully, you'll be too happily ensconced in bike riding, hiking, swimming, playing tennis, or enjoying the outdoors to notice that there is nothing new in the stores. However, if it's too hot to be outside and you venture to the mall, you might see some *long-sleeved tees* creeping onto the racks alongside a smattering of *denim* that could pass as a fall preview, along with some *lightweight sweaters*. Frankly though, that's it.

If you really can't resist a purchase, pick up a long sleeved-tee just to get yourself in the mood for cooler weather clothes, but unless you have a gaping hole in one of your spring or summer wardrobe categories that you desperately need to fill, keep your money in your pocketbook right now. In a few weeks, the stores will be packed to the gills, and you'll need every cent to be able to snap up great new stuff then. The only other money-out transaction that should happen in July (should you take your vacation) is to snap up something unique during your travels. Depending where you go and how good the local boutiques are, you may find the selection of linen shirts, dresses, bathing suits, sandals, jewelry, bags, and everything current all to be hugely different. However, just because it's different and unique and you love it, doesn't mean you need it or will be able to wear it anywhere else. Remember too, if you're at a resort destination, you won't be buying in your familiar way with the coming season in mind. Most stuff available will be resort-specific stuff, so choose wisely.

Tips for a Lower Tab

If you're lucky enough to be traveling farther afield to Europe or beyond, you should take advantage of some of the varied and wonderful local brands. It's great to have the opportunity to purchase something special. If you're heading to Europe, you should be looking at the fall preview stuff *not* the on-sale stuff. Most importantly, don't forget the dollar conversion whenever you splurge. It can make things go from expensive to out of bounds. Sometimes you can get lucky and find great purchases in your travels that even with the exchange rates don't end up being that expensive.

You may have trawled through your hometown's own lesser-priced name brand or department stores until you know the lines and the sizes left in every style. But abroad, the lesser-priced brands and department stores can reap a huge selection of different stuff. France, Italy, Spain, and the UK are the best places to do scouting in the stores that are equivalent to Macy's, Target, Wal-Mart, Miss Sixty, and so on. They have their own quirky names like Galleries Lafayette, Miss Selfridge, Asda, Marks & Spencer, Mango, and so on. Just look for the newer pieces in the stores that hint at the coming season, like the long-sleeved tees and other tops that'll work for cooler weather in fall. Ask at your hotel or someone at the tourist bureau to give you the scoop on where they're located if you don't have a friend who's local.

Unique pieces always get positive remarks from friends. Even if you're staying stateside, it's worth it to take a look around. Sometimes what I see in Dallas when I'm on the road is different from what is available in New York, and vice versa, so keep your eyes open. Sometimes the prices can be cheaper than in your hometown too, so do compare.

If you're miles from home and you just want a souvenir from your trip, okay, get a souvenir. But don't get ripped off. Don't walk directly into red-flag "tourist rip-off" territory. You may be giddy from the sun or lunchtime margaritas, but be sure you get your math straight if you're buying even a necklace on a beach boardwalk. Last, make sure you can picture yourself wearing the item out of the present context. Some things translate well, such as tunics, earrings, dresses, and even bags. But classic leather fisherman sandals bought in the Mediterranean just don't translate well anywhere else. They don't look right in Maine or in Florida or in California or on St. Barts as you think they might, even though these are all beach destinations. So think really, really hard when you pick up something unique and try to discern whether you can wear it elsewhere.

My best advice for a travel souvenir is to limit the shopping spree to inexpensive local artisan jewelry, sarongs, or belts. Whenever you wear the item or look at it at home, it will always remind you of your far-flung vacation, and no one is ever likely to have the same pieces as you. Really local stuff should not cost a bomb either as it's made locally. You will always have the special memory, too, of buying it—something special found in a foreign place. Tucked safely in your closet at home or picked out by you every day and worn repeatedly like a true basic, it's hard not to look at items bought away from home without a nice post-vacation afterglow that frankly is totally priceless!

* AUGUST *

The Right Bags, the Right Bling

Ah, the love of handbags—they're not just another fabulous accessory. Some designer handbags are lusted after, idolized, and, in some cases, given cult status (the infamous Hermès Birkin bag, with its long waiting list, for example). When the desire takes hold for these beautifully designed and crafted accessories, it's all that retailers can do to keep them in the stores. So not only is it a big deal for the consumer and the retailer, but it's big business for the designers. A lesser-known fact about the fashion industry is that large upscale fashion houses really make the big bucks when they produce a hit bag, so they try to do it every season. And it's not only about designing a great bag or hiring the most innovative designers or using the most gorgeous materials but also about making big efforts to ensure that the final products are photographed on the right celebrity. Often, too, when a large luxury fashion house produces a bag that's a big hit, the rest of that fashion house's seasonal clothing collection tends to take a backseat, but it doesn't hurt the bottom line because a hit bag is so *huge*, it invariably becomes a household name.

Of course, celebrities and their favorite bags are tough to separate! The Hermès Kelly bag once toted by Princess Grace still carries the same cache. The Kelly continues to be one of the most imitated and most expensive bags out there. Since we are all glued to the every move and whim of our modern-day celebrities, the eventual success of a particular bag can very much depend on the "right" celebrity, with the "right" bag seen about town. However, accompanied by the right celebrity or not, luxury bags influence the entire fashion food chain. Just show up at any market stall or street fair and see the hordes of those infamous knockoffs six months after their runway debuts!

Style File: Handbag Happiness

Consider this: in this body-obsessed age, bags are the *one* piece of your wardrobe that remains constant—no matter what your shape or dress size.

If you, too, are truly fanatical about your bags, you already know about the waiting lists for new products and about the difficulty of obtaining one of the coveted items that eager society girls and fashion collectors are dying to lay their hands on. The excitement and anticipation of seeing and holding a bag that has appeared on a runway but has yet to debut in the stores is hard to match.

WHICH BAG FOR EVERY DAY?

We all need a bag for every day, so we may as well love and cherish the one we use, right? But have you not noticed that lately, somehow, we all seem to need and use bigger bags? Maybe it's a result of our fast-paced lives, in which we use our bags to house not only our keys and wallet but also our laptop and maybe even our gym clothes. It could even be that more of us drag our work home (ugh!). If you do a quick historic check at vintage movies, you truly won't see anything shaped like a computer bag, backpack, overloaded satchel, or gym bag in sight! That's simply because the lifestyle and accessories from decades ago didn't demand big bags. There were no laptops and no alpha-female gym rats! Today we're all multitaskers. Our roles as mothers, workers, wives, students, and athletes all happily blur, and we just need more stuff with us each day—period. Luckily, there are ways to save your shoulders from pain and still live fashionably in the modern world if you pick the right everyday bag.

As if choosing the right bag—one that suits your life *and* looks great on you—wasn't enough of a process, there's yet *another* trend to consider: one of the latest fashion phenomena that has emerged as we crawled into this century is carrying (or using) two pocketbooks or bags each day as a matter of habit.

The right two bags?

As unusual as this may sound to you at first, if you think about it carefully, you may have already adapted to the two-bag trend without even knowing it! Take stock of your own bag situation, How many bags do you leave the house with on a typical workday? Surely, you never leave home without your all-purpose handbag for wallet, keys, and makeup, and so on. But what about your paperwork or laptop or both? Do you have an extra bag for these items? And do you perhaps have an extra tote here and there for gym clothes or your brown bag lunch? If you're already lugging multiple bags with you on a daily basis, why not get your fashion needs *and* your lifestyle needs met at the same time? Since we all seem to need a larger bag to accommodate our lives and a smaller one to help with the practicality of not having to lug a large one everywhere, I got to thinking, "Why not overhaul one's stash of pocketbooks and pair them together?"

The idea is to share the load when your load expands during the day. Select small bags to fit inside larger ones, medium sizes to go with lightweight totes, or larger fabric roll-up totes to fit inside medium-sized bags. It's best if the pairings go stylistically together as well as physically. For example, a quilted Chanel envelope clutch won't fit well inside a structured Doctor bag, but it will fit nicely inside a large black leather tote. Similarly, a large, funky combat green canvas tote will easily hold a soft hobo-style studded black leather bag.

The colors of your pairings don't need to be the same, but it helps if they're from the same family. Here's why: The idea is to be able to carry just one bag during the parts of the day when you need to (like on the way to work). Then, you have the option to use only the smaller bag containing just your essential phone, lipstick, money, ID, and keys at other points in the day, perhaps heading out to run errands, to an unexpected fancy lunch, or to dinner straight from work. The point of pairing them stylistically is that they complement your outfit, both together and apart, giving you the option to stylishly carry both bags at the same time should the need arise.

This also gives you the option to ditch your larger bag, should the need arise. Remember, always, always keep your credit cards, money, and IDs on you no matter how small your small bag is. Don't risk these to save fashion face!

Changing bags often is also part of having a modern handbag wardrobe. Even Hillary Clinton remarked on a talk show that the easiest way to change bags is always to house your small items in a mesh pouch that you can pick up from any local drugstore and place this inside your bag of choice. When it's time to switch, simply transfer the inside pouch into your ready and waiting bag. No matter which multibag philosophy you subscribe to, you'll lighten your load—literally—if you take on the big-bag, small-bag approach. And that mysterious neck pain might just go away.

HOW TO BUILD A STABLE OF BAGS

Pairing up your bags assumes that you have a collection, a stable of them even. Frankly, we should *all* have one—not necessarily a full-on *luxury* stable, but a good selection of bags that can be used for a variety of occasions.

It makes no difference if your stable comprises luxury or lesser-priced bags or even if you pair up luxury bags and lesser bags with each other for the two-bags concept. Find a time to clear out and take inventory of what you already have and make suitable pairings by laying everything out on the floor. You might even be pleasantly surprised by what you find!

Chances are you'll find you have many bags in one color, maybe brown or black, if that's what you use most. But take a good look at the collection objectively as a whole to see what might be missing. Perhaps a fabulous fun small red bag stands out and you really love it, but you don't wear it often enough as it doesn't hold much. Now you can think about the possibilities of purchasing a larger bag (maybe a denim tote?) to work with it. Don't forget to include your inventory of very small evening bags. Are they all formal, structured, and classic? Make a mental note to keep an eye out for more casual, fun, quirky versions for dressing down while still dressing up. Then do the same with the larger sizes, and see if you don't notice a gaping hole or color that might really juice up your wardrobe. But take heed: if you are really a casual dresser day in and day out, avoid the temptation to acquire formal structured bags that you simply won't wear. Be choosy when you pick out any new pocketbook, and always ask yourself, How will I wear this? If you can't imagine how while standing right there in the store or staring into the computer screen at a find on eBay, take a pass. Even though your goal is probably to acquire a bigger and better and more fabulous bag collection, there will always be one bag that's your "it" bag for now. Bet's on that it is your newest one!

You should probably have at least one status bag in your stable. Status bags are great, they are classics, and they cost a fortune, but if you can stand the expense, the investment will pay off with long-term use. Whether you stretch to this level or not is a matter between you and your credit card! Personally, I often covet the designer name brand bags like Prada or Gucci, but truth be told, lesser label bags that are modestly priced do the job just as well if selected carefully.

If you do purchase a designer bag that costs a bomb, treat it as you would a new pair of expensive sunglasses or boots, and style the rest of your wardrobe around it for maximum use. This way you will get to wear it every day.

The good news is that your one status bag need not be new or costly, and it does not have to be from the current season. It could easily be sourced from a consignment store or from a vintage resale store. Either way, style your outfits with it as the focus, and your "special" bag will work hard for you repeatedly.

How to Type Bags

There are many different types of bags out there, from the fakes on the street to the pre-season, pre-runway styles gifted in advance to top magazine editors and celebrities before general launch. Most of us can't afford the luxury-designer "it" styles of the season that are super pricey, but thankfully, taking the focus away from these, there are a huge variety of other shopping options that are sure to net you the best bag. Here they are in decreasing price order.

Designer bags

At the top of the pile are the luxury label bags we all see in magazines that retail for thousands of dollars. And sometimes tens of thousands!

Below them, however, there is a huge section of the market of lesser-labeled bags, still large well-known names, that are more modestly priced, though sometimes extending into the hundreds of dollars.

Look-alike bags

Next, down the price scale are the brilliant and completely affordable look-alike bags. Sometimes overlooked, a look-alike bag with a name you may or may not have heard of will have stylish details or features that *remind* you of the very expensive luxury designers' styles. These are a great category to look for.

Fakes

The fakes by comparison are simply a blatant copy of luxury bags and come out as bad clones of an exact designer style. The name or logo is often cloned too, but the entire product is fabricated using inferior-quality materials.

Designer vs. look-alike vs. fake

If luxury designer pocketbooks and their price tags are primarily lotto-winning fantasy purchases and the fakes are what the fashion police (and the fair trade, copyright, and labor unions) would lock you up for, the look-alike bags start to look very good. Thankfully, this category of mid-priced bags often offers the largest selection and variety out there.

Why look-alike bags are okay!

What do I mean by look-alike bags? Maybe you've seen these bags, maybe you haven't. If you live on a tight budget, these are the bags you should be keeping an eye out for. They're the incredibly well priced accessories available at department stores like the brand Worthington available at JCPenny or slightly more expensive bags that carry the name of a clothing designer like Betsey Johnson. Obviously, either a Worthington or a Betsey Johnson bag is likely to cost about one fiftieth of a Gucci price tag!

You will know you have come across a good look-alike bag because the designers or design teams that produce them are fashion forward in their thinking, and the results are great interpretations incorporating the current (or upcoming seasons) trend details without copying stitch for stitch. Really good bags that fall into this category are typically hard to place. But they look authentic. They may have Marc Jacobs–style buckles and hardware or the leather cross-stitch is reminiscent of Luella Bartley or a shape that is popular from the Jimmy Choo line. But even though it is easy to spot these influences, they are executed slightly differently from the real thing. The cool part for you is to scour your local department store and even if you have never heard of some of the brands, hone in on styles that give you the same style satisfaction without the price tag.

Always keep in mind the details that you love from the high-end designer versions (perhaps the color combo and topstitching). One more thing: the upshot of finding a great look-alike bag that satisfies is that if it is made out of less-expensive materials, it is likely to be less heavy than the real thing, a certain plus when we all carry around too much stuff to begin with.

Why can't I buy a fake?

We've all seen fake bags on sale for reasonable prices from street vendors—bags that strategically say "Pravda" instead of Prada or "Chanet" instead of Chanel. As tempting as they are, please, please, please stay away from these cheap knockoffs. Unfortunately, many of these are illegal and usually trace back to dodgy production in rural places where labor laws and copyright laws are broken with abandon. More and more street bags are being seized by authorities, and although imitation is the most sincere form of flattery, there are now serious implications for buying and selling these wares. This aside, there are actually very few really, *really* good fakes available that imitate the designer styles so well, so it's not such a big loss.

Style File

Despair not over fake designer bags! With a practiced eye, you can get a fantastic look-alike bag that will be totally legit, totally legal, and totally under budget.

WHAT IS A RIGHT-HAND RING?

Another brand new (and most liberating!) concept in accessories is the selecting and wearing of the right-hand ring, a focus piece that draws oohs and aahs and attention for its sheer beauty and is unburdened with the emotional and sentimental significance of an engagement ring. Worn on the fourth finger of the right hand, a sparkly right-hand ring is a genius idea and not-so-guilty pleasure that applies to singles and marrieds alike. In fact, if you've not met Mr. Right, why not buy your own sparkly rock from the increasing selection of large-scale fashion baubles. It's an ingenious concept that allows you to choose your own special piece of jewelry that you feel great wearing.

So how to choose a fabulous right-hand ring? It's all about what you love! Maybe you already know what you like or your skin tone looks great with rubies or sapphires. Remember when Nicole Kidman showed up to the Oscars in maharajah gold and enamel jewelry that perfectly complemented her chartreuse-colored dress and red hair? My friend celebrity jeweler Martin Katz created the "wow" factor for Nicole with the exquisite jewelry that night, but there might be a combo that is always a hit on you. Maybe you are a sterling silver purist—anything goes. You can pick your ring according to your birthstone, your semi-precious jewel preferences, or simply pick something you just love.

If you already own a ring with a gorgeous stone but a less-than-gorgeous setting, this is the moment to design your dream ring. Take it to your favorite jeweler and get it remodeled! Whether you're playing the trendsetter or the style icon, remodeling old jewelry allows you to create something that is incredibly, uniquely you!

Unclear about what to pick? Maybe you need help determining your jewelry personality. The most modern way to wear all jewelry, real or fake, is to mix everything up and wear it with confidence.

The six (tongue-in-cheek) jewelry personalities— which one are you?

See if you fit into the jewelry personalities in the proceeding section to refocus your ideas for a desirable right-hand ring or to figure out if your jewelry box is working to help you express yourself! I'll take a bet you can recognize some if not all the *types*. Just remember, too, that accessory fads come and go, but the joy of jewelry is that pieces kept can be recycled and mixed with other pieces later. And after all, jewelry doesn't take up much storage space.

1. **The European.** You just *know* this type from a mile off. She looks like money!—but *understated* money. You know if you're this type because your confidence is high. You'll also know if you aspire to this type because you yearn for this type of effortless chic whenever you see it walk by! The good news is that if you study closely, it's easy to imitate. To adopt the look of the European successfully, pay attention to the core of her Mediterranean and Jet-Set chic: a gold Cartier tank watch or other clean classic modern bracelet watch. Her hands are adorned with simple (sometimes multiple) white, rose, or pink gold tennis bracelets or classic bangles.

   With the European, it's always about the gold. Gold coins or crosses or perhaps linked gold wedding rings worn around the neck. Gold chains are also a big part of this style. Large or small gold hoop earrings are a fixture too, but only in the right proportions to hair length (long hair with big hoops, short hair with small).

Stick to all things gold and all things classic, and if you aren't loaded with cash, keep to simple and minimal. The European is an especially good look to try out if you don't feel that you have a distinct "jewelry personality." PS: This look really works great on olive or darker skins.

2. **The Goth.** Black and religious pieces such as stunning bejeweled crosses are the core pieces of the modern Goth. But the Goth personality does not necessarily pair her statement jewelry with distressed rags or deconstructed clothes. She can be a clean, modern, sophisticated Goth! Armfuls of Lucite bangles and jet and anthracite chokers do feature heavily, but light- and dark-colored baubles, beads, and bangles or leather bracelets or other unusual materials get equal treatment. If you're going for the Goth look, remember the cardinal rule: layer, layer, layer.

3. **The Princess.** The Princess loves her flash. She wears a lot of jewelry all the time and sometimes has to take one piece off after she's loaded herself up. Even she knows she can overdo it! Her jewelry box is fun to play with and brings instant happiness to all who open it. Her rocks and jewels are her babies. She's always turned out in rings, bangles, baubles, earrings, and necklaces that are colorful, are studded with sapphires, rubies, and emeralds (or imitation colored stones that mimic them), and feature rocks that are large, large, large. She wears both gold and silver and loves her well-worn status pieces like the Tiffany charm bracelet in sterling silver. Often the colors of the stones flatter each other and the colors of her clothes, shoes, and hair. She constantly wears pinks, blues, topaz, and gold. Diamonds make her shiver. They are so exciting,

but in a pinch, cubic zirconium works just fine too. As long as it sparkles and shines, the Princess is happy.

4. **The Modernist**. The Modernist seeks out the unusual, handmade, sculptural, wearable art pieces. Be it a bangle bought on the street at a craft fair or a highly stylized pair of 18-karat asymmetrical earrings, each piece that she wears is unique and has a sculptural or "designer" story behind it.

Sometimes rare or raw natural materials like amber or jade fit into her jewelry box, but it's never in an earthy way as the Modernist is always very polished. Unusual metals like stainless steel or copper often adorn the Modernist's wrists, and entire outfits can be planned around these architectural acquisitions. Often a Modernist uses clothing as a blank canvas on which to showcase her jewelry. The Modernist look is very cool, and though it's not for everyone, it works astoundingly well if you can pull it off.

5. **The Gypsy**. Beads of every size, shape, and weight feature prominently in this boho-chic style. Jewelry embellished with glass and vintage beads and brightly colored threads and tassels of every size jangle happily alongside bundles of noisy bangles. The Gypsy has adornments for every part of her body. She, of all the jewelry personalities, is most likely to wear a belly chain, an ankle chain, rings on her fingers and toes, and a sparkler in her belly button! She may have a penchant for Southwestern or other culturally inspired pieces. The Gypsy's style is never constant. One day she appears adorned with long beads and tassels to accessorize a long flowing dress; another day her crisp white shirt with jeans deliberately sets off a bright blue turquoise and sterling silver necklace.

6. **The Romantic.** Hers is a vintage lot. The Romantic usually favors earlier decades over current ones—perhaps Victorian, Deco, forties, or seventies—and has a collection of vintage pieces or antiques or imitations from those periods in time. She may have an affinity for items made from bone, celluloid, wood, ivory, or plastic, depending on her favorite time period. Some of her pieces are valuable and collectible, or they are even heirlooms. Most essentially, she sees her jewelry not just as a fashion accessory but as an accrued collection that increases in value as a group. The Romantic also knows her jewels, including when and where they were likely made. The pieces that comprise her jewelry personality may even be the mainstay of her style icon status for which she is known. She certainly delights in wearing her signature pieces over and over again. Anyone can pick an era of vintage jewelry to wear and collect (it's not always expensive). Make it your own by mixing with individual wardrobe choices.

The hybrid

Can't find a way to find a fit with any of the jewel profiles? Then create one of your own! Maybe you're that unique. Good for you if you are. Go ahead and create a name for your profile. Maybe you're a *Princess-Goth* or *Mod-European* hybrid. But no matter what you are, the key is to recognize your likes and dislikes and to stick to your theme. Chances are that if you collect items that speak to you and look good on your arms, ears, and décolletage, you will love, cherish, and wear them forever.

HOW TO BUILD YOUR
WATCH WARDROBE

Did you ever find yourself all dressed up looking good, but then you add your watch and it looks wrong? This is why every woman needs a watch wardrobe—a selection of watches that match your mood, your destination, and your outfit, which is most important. A watch is as much an accessory as anything else you put on, and it should be treated like any other jewelry choice. Look at your watch right now. Does it fit what you're wearing? Or is it just your way of telling

Style File: Budget Accessories

You can be the queen of cheap, but with a good eye, you can get away with looking like a million bucks. Prowl your local vintage shops and flea markets for pieces that have some weight to them but that aren't so shiny. They should *look* vintage and weathered, so if they are tarnished when you find them, don't clean them up overenthusiastically.

time? Does it go on every day no matter what you put on? Is it sometimes too heavy or too spindly looking to wear with some of your favorite outfits? Does it go with everything you wear *every single day?* Really? If it does, congrats! You must already have achieved style icon status. Just like shoes, it's rare that one watch will work perfectly for every dressing occasion. What works while gardening (or is suited for this) is likely different from what you may prefer to wear to work or out to a formal function.

Building a watch wardrobe depends on your budget, but there is really no need to spend a fortune just to have a good selection. Most of us have one type of watch that works for us most of the time. If you work in a corporate environment, this is likely to be a classic watch with a metal or leather strap. If you're a creative type and are still in school or work in a casual environment, you may have something fun or unusual that works most days. It's not hard to build your reserve of watches from reasonably priced brands in no time.

If you do own an expensive luxury watch as your main watch, it doesn't mean that an inexpensive additional item to build up the wardrobe is out of the question. Even if your preference is only for luxury high-quality timepieces and you'd prefer to have a smaller collection of luxury items than a larger one of fashion watches, sometimes it's nice to have one timepiece that you don't have to worry about. You'll be surprised how much fun it is to put on a sporty watch instead of your usual timepiece when you're next dressing to play tennis or golf. And if you select well, chances are that you'll receive multiple compliments on the new timepieces appearing every now and again on your wrist. Change is good. The funny thing is, if you're known among your friends for owning and wearing a luxury watch most of the time, those around you will assume that the different timepieces starting to appear on occasion are just as exclusive! It's how you wear your watch that counts, of course.

Because a watch is very much a noticeable accessory, it helps mix things up and create flexibility with your outfits. If you are wearing only jeans, a plain white shirt, and a pair of flats, a dressy watch goes a long way to making your look deliberately understated chic. Similarly, if your day dress is silk and dressy, adding your fun watch and a pair of casual shoes will go a long way to bringing it down a notch or two. Watches can be worn with a touch of irony, so just try it on! Once you have started a small watch wardrobe, try them on with different outfits and you will see what I mean.

If you're not concerned with luxury brands or authenticity, cruise eBay for fun, interesting, even quasi-vintage watches that are different and quirky. As long as they're in working order and you like the way they look, you'll enjoy them as part of your watch wardrobe. Just because you're technically a *grown-up* doesn't mean you can't pair a fun vintage Mickey Mouse watch with your favorite pair of sweats on Saturday!

Depending on what you own already, increase your watch wardrobe by adding one watch from each of the four style-type categories in the following list. It's a pretty fail-safe way to begin a collection:

Style Note: Take a Risk

One more thing: casting against type (wearing something unexpected on you according to your taste, position, job, or age) can also be a stylish alternative to your everyday accessories. Keep 'em guessing!

1. **Sporty:** Choose something colorful, preferably waterproof, lightweight, and cool (in temperature) to wear. Perhaps something set on a fabric or rubber bracelet that comes loaded with interchangeable watch faces.

2. **Dressy:** Choose something with a metallic bracelet, maybe a jewel or two sparkling out from the face or bezel (the part that surrounds the face) and keep the bracelet part skinny, dainty, and manageable.

3. **Chic:** Something with a classic gold or silver face, be it sterling silver, 18-karat gold, or simply inexpensive chrome or silver-plated metal—whatever your budget. Keep it to something simple that is adorned with a classic leather strap and has roman or other simple

numerals. Size is less important—large or small—than proportion. It must look imposing and smart on you.

4. *Fun:* This is where you get to play with colored snake-skin, faux alligator, and whatever materials your crazy heart desires. Maybe try something big or playful and trendy or something for the moment—even a quasi-vintage cartoon watch.

WHAT TO SHOP IN AUGUST

* Winter coats
* Back to school
* Winter boots
* Winter skirts
* Flats
* Denims

It might be August and you are dripping in sweat, but I'm urging you to clear off the beach, get out of the pool, and step away from those wine coolers. It's time to get into serious shopping mode!

Now's the time to shop for *winter coats*. Yes, you heard that right. It may seem crazy, but when you heed this advice and hit the lovely air-conditioned quiet and peaceful stores, you'll understand the logic. The winter coat racks are just in—waiting for you—with every size in every color available. It's a beautiful thing. Just try them on! You'll be able to see what the trends for the season are and decide if you're going to jump into the fray, or you might get sticker shock and decide to dig out your oldest coats from storage and see how they'll fare as reruns. But no matter what, this exercise will start you planning your fall outfits and not a moment too soon. By trying on coats, you get a preview of how the season's styles fit you, and you can give yourself ample time to figure out what your main choice for winter warmth will be right now before the mercury drops.

Of course, once you are back to cruising the stores, you are going to see the multitude of fabulous fall stuff that is merchandised as back-to-school offerings. Believe it or not, the first smattering of *winter boots* and *winter skirts* will have arrived too. Because fall means there is a lot of running around to do with back-to-school events, there is a huge selection of flats to be found. Go get 'em while the selection is still big! Right now there is a huge denim push, so check them out and head full-on into purchasing something from the new loads of *fresh jeans.* These may have accents that are trend led for the season or simply a new take on the classics. If you are short on cash and not desperate to update this part of your wardrobe yet, you can hold off if you do not see your dream pair, as there will be new deliveries later in the season too.

HOW TO BUY JEANS

Since jeans are essentially the glue that joins our entire wardrobe together, it goes without saying that getting the right pairs is *quintessential* to your wardrobe. But how many pairs do you actually need? And how do you shop for them? "Jeans are here to stay," says "Boogie" Weinglass, my own personal denim guru and the former president and CEO of Merry Go Round—a chain he started in the 1970s and built from one store to fifteen hundred all specializing in jeans. Boogie still sells jeans everyday from his five stores in Aspen, Colorado. He knows only too well the conundrums facing his customers. "Jeans are quite hard to buy," he says. "You really have to buy jeans based on your body type." But is there an actual formula? And how do you know when you've made the right style choices?

Here's his hit list for doing it right in denim:

1. **Ask for sales help.** The staff members in specialty denim stores know their brands and all the various different cuts of jeans. Tell the sales associate what you need for your wardrobe and let that person know if you are hankering after dark denim, light denim, clean pressed denim, or denim with lots of holes and frays.

2. **Remember *how* previous brands fit you.** And tell the sales help which brands you have worn in the past. Every major denim line has its own fit within the line, and although all the lines are updated frequently, the basic styles do stay the same. If one brand fit you before, it will likely fit you again.

3. **Look for jeans based on your body type.** Again, this is where a helpful sales staff comes in handy. If there is no sales help, you will need to be your own stylist. And for the most flattering fit, you will need to consider body shape over what's trendy. There are two basic types of jeans: low rise and high rise. This is the height that the jean extends upward on your tummy from the crotch.

4. **Just try them on!** All jeans fit differently, and so much of finding the perfect pair is trial and error. Start with four or five pairs. Ask the sales help to bring you new styles, and then assess each one and decide what's not working. Come out of the fitting room and let others see. Other shoppers' reactions are helpful. Some people make the worst decisions being isolated in a closed-in fitting room. It's too easy to give up finding the right pair without feedback on alternative sizing or

The Right Jeans for You

A buying guide to the best jeans for your body type:

If you have a flat tummy, you can wear low-rise jeans. In general, the thinner you are, the lower the rise you can get away with. And the lower the rise, the taller you'll look.

If you are heavier set or proud to show off a bigger tummy, pick a medium or high-rise jean.

If your thighs are thicker, you may want to pick a darker color for a slimming effect. Remember, too, that heavy denim is more forgiving on heavier legs.

If you have a large butt, select jeans with a basic pocket, not a fancy pocket that draws attention. Don't ever pick something with really low pockets as they tend to draw the eye downward, creating the effect of a bigger lower butt. You should know, too, that cheaper jeans companies use the same size pocket on all their jeans. In truth, however, your butt will look best if you pick a brand that changes pocket size proportionally to jeans size even if they're more expensive.

If you have over a 29-inch waist (or more than a size 6), don't wear skinny jeans. The proportions don't work well above this clothing size. Instead, a boot-cut jean (flared slightly past the knee) with a mid-rise in dark denim will be the most flattering.

appearance. Unlike shopping for swimwear, which is best kept between you and your favorite salesperson, it's a bonus to take a real friend along when shopping for jeans. With jeans you need the extra opinion—especially the "rear view" opinion!

5. **Do they fit you? Be pragmatic.** The perfect fit shouldn't be skintight, but shouldn't have wrinkles or gaps anywhere either. When jeans are too tight around the waist, your tummy spills over, and it may mean you should try some that are higher in the back. If they gap in the waist when you bend over showing your butt to everyone, that's not good either. A good fit is when you bend down and you can't see your butt below the back waistband. If they fit really well, there will be no puckering anywhere. The only place jeans should ever pucker is down by the ankle. If it fits in the butt, doesn't gap in the waist, and isn't too tight in the crotch, you know you've found the right pair.

6. **Features affect function.** The opening at the bottom of the jeans leg ranges from 12 inches (a very skinny pencil jean) to 15 to 16 inches (a boot cut). If you plan to show off new boots, you'll need a pair that's skinny enough to tuck in. So ironically, skinny jeans are better for showing off boots than boot-cut jeans. Remember that the tighter the jeans are through your knees, the taller and skinnier you look but the harder it is to sit down! Very tight jeans are very sexy, but you'll definitely sacrifice some comfort. If you can, go for jeans with 2 percent Lycra or stretch in them. You'll still get that tight fit but with more comfort and give. Four-way stretch is the new advanced and amazing technology hitting the jean scene. It doesn't give as much as cotton, but it stretches all four ways so you can move and bend. If you can find a jean with four-way stretch incorporated that flatters you—get them.

Consider doing alterations. Even the best-fitting jeans sometimes need extra help. The most common jean alteration is hemming the leg length. All good jean brands make their styles to fit tall people! So don't be put off by the extra long leg length in a well-fitting jean, just get a good tailor to bring them up to your own personalized length. The second most common alteration is taking in the waist. If you have muscular thighs but a skinny waist, you'll inevitably need to do alterations. Remember that when you're trying on your jeans at the tailor's to wear the same footwear you expect to wear with your jeans, and keep in mind that it's more sophisticated to wear your jeans as long as you possibly can without tripping over them (in heels or flats).

HOW TO BUILD A BLUE JEAN WARDROBE

So how do you build a stable of jeans? And how many do you need? How long is a piece of string? You could easily have a fully functioning jeans wardrobe by owning just five pairs.

1. **Your Everyday Pair**: This is likely to be your most used pair. Search for a slim boot-cut pair in a mid-blue denim with no rips that is tight in the knee and widens from the knee to the ground. These are very versatile, should be worn every day, are perfect with boots, and should be worn over your boots.

2. **Your Classic Pair**: Pick a dark sophisticated denim or a raw color in a straight leg cut with a 14-inch opening at the bottom of the leg. These are the easiest jeans to dress up for evening or to wear at more dressy jeans-suitable events.

3. **Your Trendy Pair**: As long as the trend suits your body type, get what's in. The fashiony element may be an

embellishment or finish like rhinestones, embroidery, fraying, or paint splattering. Or the trend could be a shape, like the skinny leg or very baggy silhouette. Wear your trendy jeans immediately when you get them and while they're hot, but drop them the instant they're not! PS: Beware that very trendy jeans packed for a trip may limit your styling. The trendy features may scream out so loud, you won't be able to mix and match so well, and it'll be obvious you wore the same pair every day!

4. **Your Trouser-Style Pair:** These are versatile jeans to wear when the occasion really calls for something more formal but you don't feel like dressing up. They could be a thin summer-weight denim, perhaps with a tab front and a slouchy, looser fit, almost palazzo pant style. The color could also be light making them good for warm summer weather.

5. **Your In-Love Pair:** This is the spare pair that you fall in love with and can't live without. It might be a duplication of one of the just-mentioned pairs, the same brand and style, but with the hem of the legs brought up to a different length to wear with three-inch heels instead of flats. Or it could be a pair that is Capri length (finishes at the calf) or a pair you like to wear rolled up from the ankle or with unusual styling like cargo pockets.

If you have bought jeans in accordance with the hot hints just listed and they fit great, whatever you do, don't ever throw them out. If the fit is still great and they continue to look good, keep them. The only times to discard jeans are when trendy jeans are out or when they get holes in them that are not flattering or if your body shape changes. Consider, too, that you can easily recycle jeans. You might wear them a different way, like cropped to shorts or cropped and rolled up or altered and turned into skirts or even a bag! You can also change a pair of jeans drastically that look too short. Simply unpick the hem and leave the fraying raw edge to skim over your shoes. You'll gain an extra three quarters of an inch in length.

TIPS FOR A LOWER TAB

Since August is a time for possible heavy expenditures, you may be feeling a whole lot poorer right now! Don't panic. Really nice coats especially sometimes eat up a hefty chunk of change, but they're worth it as they can last a good long time. Thankfully, they don't need replacing every year if you buy well.

Since you figured out your jewelry personality in this chapter, it's a good time to mention that thrift stores, flea markets, street fairs, and antique markets are all great alternative sources for building up your jewelry box. Make sure though, if you are after acquiring some valuable vintage pieces, that you buy from a reputable and established dealer. If you hanker for budget baubles, pick a collection of fun stuff from one vendor, and then, bargain and barter your way into a knockdown deal! My personal favorites for acquiring new jewelry are garage sales and estate sales. Sometimes families have a big estate sale and really throw the baby out with the bathwater (so to speak). If you have the patience for this sort of shopping, you just might find yourself a unique vintage steal. I found a fabulous, fabulous right-hand ring at a garage sale. Okay, it may not be worth much, but it *looks* the business on me.

A really great site for watches is eBay, but please do learn about what you're purchasing and *read* the sellers' rules just in case you don't get what you were expecting. Department stores have the safest return policies for buying middle- and lower-priced fashion watches, and the selection is usually huge, so don't think you have to narrow your search to a watch-dedicated store.

If you've inherited a valuable watch that's not quite for you, sometimes a jewelry dealer might take it in part exchange for something else. But do think carefully about giving up things that may be of sentimental value, now or in the future, as you may regret it. Seller's remorse is no fun!

As far as buying coats and boots at full retail the minute they hit the stores, you may not save directly on the price tag if you buy now, but if you see something that you truly love, go for it. You'll save yourself so much time (and that's worth money!) in the long run. Think carefully about what's missing from your coat choices and think about your wardrobe with a broad mind. For example, if you live in girly-girl dresses no matter what the winter weather, then make your coat purchase fit your style. You might even wear a dress to go shopping. And if you, like me, are very short, watch the length of your coat; a long one can be too, too much. By the end of August, your perfect coat choice will be hanging in your closet and your own personal winter theme will be taking shape, which is how you save—by *not* purchasing other mistake pieces of clothing that won't work with your newly formulated style. You won't need to spend again on anything like this for some time.

Once you've got your blueprint, the other apparel choices are easy to fit together. If you really need to save a buck or two on a special coat or pair of boots, check online for online retailers' prices. Mixing an expensive coat with lesser-priced items works just great. This taps into the concept we'll get into in the October chapter—mixing high end with low end. When you anchor your look by splurging on a few very cool pieces and blending these with a few great budget items, you simply save in the end. Coats are one of those big splurge choices you sometimes have to make.

* SEPTEMBER *

Get a Shoe In!

Shoes—the one iconic item for the closet that keeps women shopping all day long. Why do women love shoes so much? Perhaps because they're so versatile and so forgiving. Even when your body size changes, shoe size doesn't necessarily follow. I think we can safely say that shoes are the world's most fantasized about fashion item. And adding the fetishism surrounding women's shoes and men, it's easy to see why they're the sexiest fashion item too. No wonder women feel their fashion power strongest through their footwear. The only problem is that gorgeous shoes have a habit of flying off the Richter scale in price, not to mention the comfort level (or lack thereof). Who hasn't tried on a pair of shoes that looks out of this world but unfortunately feels like a medieval torture device? Some pairs, alas, are better just to look at than to wear. You probably have a couple of pairs like those in your closet right now. I know I have pairs carefully stashed in the closet I've barely worn that start up an unresolved emotional conflict each time the box is opened. Boo hoo!

Fortunately, high style, high comfort, and high price tags—at least in shoes—are three very random realities.

Paradoxically, you can get all three in the same shoe or none at all.

HOW TO BUY BUDGET SHOES
WITH HIGH STYLE

Of course, the ideal pair of shoes has high style, high comfort, and low price tags. And it's a tall order sometimes when outrageous new trends or special must-have details prevent your shoe fantasies from becoming a reality! But armed with a strict list of criteria for your search, you can make the ultimate attempt to find the ideal combination that satisfies your soles, your stylish sensibilities, and your available stash of cash.

Here's a checklist, point by point, to help put you on the right track:

Know what you like—and what's in style: Study the styles and shapes of the most current high-end shoes. This can be done in one very quick scan of the current glossy magazines or from a trip to the mall. When you see a desirable and very expensive pair of shoes in a luxury store, stop to take note in your mind exactly what it is about them that you like. Perhaps you love country-like gingham or the strictness of patent leather. Or maybe it's the shape of the heel that looks new and fresh, and suddenly you recognize this as a trend because you've seen other brands produce something with similar details.

Hit the budget stores: Go first to large discount shoe superstores like Famous Footwear, DSW, or even Payless if you can, all of which offer a wide variety of choices and brands to choose from. You can always go to your town's mid-priced boutiques to see their offerings too.

Look for luxury details: Once inside, go look for replications of the details that you liked on the luxury brands. You may or may not find them on styles that you love. For example, you may find gingham on flats rather than on wedges or patent on d'Orsay pumps but not on flats. It is not a perfect world, but knowing the details you like and seeking them out is a good place to start. Keep an open mind, though—you might just see something unexpected along the way. Pick just one detail to focus your search on. This way you will end up being very discriminating, and this is great for when you are shopping through a huge number of styles.

Make sure they suit your feet: Just try them on! Do you feel as excited about them now that they are on you? You can determine if a shoe looks great on you by standing sideways in the mirror to get your foot and leg profile and then by standing with your back to the mirror and craning your neck to see the back view. Do the shoes elongate your legs by creating an uninterrupted stretch of skin upward toward your knees? Or do the straps look too clunky and shorten the look of your legs? If your ankles are not slim, a very tight ankle strap may not flatter your foot and legs very well. Maybe your dainty or petite ankles look disproportionate in stacked heavy wedges when viewed from the side? Consider the view from all angles. If they're comfortable and if you like what you see—slam down that plastic!

Check if they are uncomfortable: Does it matter to
you? Can you wear them for outings where you
would not need to be on your feet much? Do
you love them enough that you could use them
infrequently as limo shoes—a term describing a
pair of shoes that may only be worn when you
have door-to-door transportation and there is zero
chance of any table dancing!

Take a pass: If it does not matter to you that they are
uncomfortable or they are not *unbearable* and they
are *really* under budget, go ahead, get 'em. But if
you are planning to wear them a lot, take a pass.
You will find something else that fits better with
similar or better style accents.

WHY UNCOMFORTABLE SHOES
WILL NOT EVER CHANGE

There's no big mystery surrounding shoes that are uncomfortable in the beginning. Either they are or they aren't. Just
know that they don't *become* comfortable later. Not ever. It
doesn't matter if they're budget or luxury shoes, the way
they feel on you those first few moments is the way they'll
feel forever. Take this to heart and remember it when you
go shopping for shoes.

Budget shoes *especially* don't change, as they're usually
made from man-made materials not natural leathers and
suede that have a very small amount of "give." If you're
looking for comfort in a shoe, the most important thing is
that new shoes are wearable from the first moment you put
them on. Of course, any worn on the first outing may rub
or give blisters, even though they seemed comfortable in
the store—there's no safeguard against this. Heel pads, gel

pads, insoles, or other additions can help protect pressure points. Pressure on any one part of the foot is no fun, and inserts can work great. Dr. Scholl's has made an equal name for itself supplying footpad accessories and manufacturing and designing shoes that don't shred the feet.

After years of styling on television with all manner of designer high- and low-end shoes, I found myself working fairly consistently with Aerosoles (it is a company that only makes comfy trend-conscious shoes). They are responsible for teaching me shoe comfort 101. Here is my take on it!

WHAT YOU WILL LEARN FROM SUSAN'S SHOE COMFORT 101

Let's face it. If you went to your closet to seek out your truly most comfortable shoes, they'd likely be your sneakers, right? That's probably because they're made of soft and supple materials and they fit supportively under the arch and around the ankle when laced up. Also, over time they mold to your feet like a second skin. Sadly, few fashion-forward shoes wear in this way. But armed with a little knowledge about why those pinching, rubbing styles are so hard to wear, it's possible to select some that have both form and function you can live with.

* *Every foot is different.* All of us have widely ranging different-shaped feet—even those of us who share the same size. It goes without saying that if every foot is different, not every shoe fits every foot.

* *A shoe mold doesn't change.* The shape of a shoe mold, which is the blueprint for a shoe, doesn't flex. So, if your foot doesn't fit right away, it never will. That's why some shoes feel "stiff" and will always hurt

you. You should try another style with a similar look that fits your foot better.

* ***The angle of the "last" is key.*** This determines the gradient between the highest and lowest point of the shoe. In other words, it's how high your heels are. The best kind of last eliminates burning on the ball of the foot even in a high heel as it prevents the foot from being thrust forward. A comfortable shoe is all about equal distribution of weight so you feel like you're standing naturally. There's a universal process (used, for example, by Aerosoles) to help improve comfort and fit. That's what they call product development, and it's all about how the shoe's last or mold is made. Whether buying a high or low heel, if the shoe doesn't make the foot sit at the correct angle, it'll hurt.

* ***Better-quality leather gives a richer look.*** If you want mid-priced shoes that look more expensive, look for shoes that are made with better-quality leather. You can often determine this by the density of pigment color. Look for rich depth of color and shine, but avoid anything that's too shiny or glossy (unless it's patent leather). Magazines that advertise very expensive shoes are a great "look book" to see and appreciate what quality leather (albeit photographed) looks like up close! Fashion magazines also give you perfect current style references like whether the in buckles are gold or chrome.

* ***Natural materials should be chosen over man-made whenever possible.*** Comparing budget shoes to luxury shoes usually means looking at man-made materials versus natural materials. Components used in very inexpensive shoes are likely to be man-made materials like imitation leather (you've probably heard it referred to as pleather) and thus don't breathe as well as shoes

made from natural fibers. Therefore, they are sometimes, but not always, the least comfortable.

＊ *Signs of quality enhance the shoe.* Telltale signs of
good-quality low-priced shoes are quite obvious. If a
pair of shoes is inexpensive but has leather soles, hand
beading, or leather lining on the inside, you have a
winner!

＊ *The really uncomfortable shoes can affect your health.*
Long-term bad back pain, bunions needing surgery,
fallen arches (as you become more flat-footed), and
pinched nerves all create problems. Not to mention the
scowly look of pain (and the wrinkles that appear)
constantly on your face when you wear treacherous
shoes! That's not beautifying either.

WHAT'S AVAILABLE WHEN

The two most important months in a shoe merchandiser's
calendar are August (for boots and fall deliveries) and early
March when the first sandals arrive. Once these big collections are released, many smaller deliveries are made that
contain styles designed to carry across the seasons. These
are known as transitional products and are suitable for wearing in the upcoming five to six months ahead, say early
spring going forward into summer.

In Aerosoles stores, the new spring styles arrive in January and February, setting the trends for the rest of the
season. If the trend is for beading or specific embellishments, then the flats, pumps, and walking shoes that arrive
now will all feature these details. By March the shoes that
arrive will look less heavy, will have more details and
cutouts, will cover less of your foot, and will be appropriate

to wear as the weather warms slightly. The very first sandals of the year arrive now too.

The market for transitional products is larger than ever, so merchandizers are designing shoes to accommodate the wants of the consumer (you and me)—stuff that is fresh and new but can be worn throughout all seasons.

Style File: *Transitional Marketing*

Because of transitional marketing, it's likely that you'll see fall-inspired shoes arriving in the stores in July. But if you prefer to save and can wait till September, there'll be plenty of fresh offerings.

A *year in the life of a shoe store*

The good news is that now that transitional styles are so available, you are not locked down into any one month to make your critical shoe purchases.

January–February: New spring-inspired collections. Wintry shoes like pumps and boots but in lighter colors and with hints of spring in the details.

March: Opened up or less-closed shoes for *Spring* that are fabricated in less heavy materials and cover less of the foot. These won't be quite as lightweight as sandals, but getting close!

April: Open-toe sandals for *Summer.*

May–June: *Transitional* products with fall in mind— dress shoes, new open toes, new casuals, and so on.

July–August: Start of closed-up *Fall* footwear like full pumps, full round toes, platforms, and tall boots.

September: *Winter* boots.

October–December: Sneaker-inspired sporty products, fur-trimmed boots, full-on winter gum bottoms, holiday metallic dress shoes, and styles that are more *Transitional* to carry through spring.

As you can see, even with the many deliveries a shoe store gets throughout the year, they don't break from the four main categories of spring, summer, fall, and winter. It's only the delivery of the transitional styles that are new additions to the calendar.

HOW TO BUY SHOES—PERIOD

Whether you plan to buy your dream pair of wedding shoes or just a great bargain pair of trend-setting stilettos for Saturday night, the following shoe-buying tips are good for all.

* ✳ *Shop late in the afternoon:* As the day goes on, your feet swell, thus they are at their largest in the late afternoon. Trying on shoes then will prevent you from buying a pair that will only fit first thing in the morning but will get more uncomfortable and tighter as the day wears on. And—it bears mentioning again—if the shoes are not comfortable in the first few minutes, even seconds, they never will be. Do not try to convince yourself that you can wear them in. No! You may have to pass up several adorable pairs of shoes in the process, but your patience in finding the right style coupled with the right comfort level at the right price is ultimately worth the search.

* ✳ *Don't try just one:* When trying on your chosen pair or pairs, be sure to put on *both* shoes and walk around a

bit. Sometimes one foot is larger than the other, so you need to know that you can tolerate both shoes on at the same time too.

* *Keep it consistent:* Make sure you're trying on both shoes *exactly* the way you would if you owned them already. For example, if you usually wear boots with socks, be sure to try on the boots with socks. If you typically wear them with stocking feet, try them on with stocking feet. And if you're trying on sandals, please, please do so with bare feet.

* *Dress to fit the shoe.* Make sure you have on the appropriate attire that allows you to see the whole effect of the shoe. If you are buying shoes that you expect to wear with a skirt, be sure you are wearing a skirt. If you are buying boots to go with your current favorite jeans, be sure to go shopping wearing those jeans to be certain that the height of the boots works with the hem.

* *Don't duplicate until you know they're perfect!* Whether you're buying luxury or budget styles, when you think you've found the perfect pair, it's hard not to buy them in every color or a second pair for backup while they still have your size. But don't. Not yet. Wear your new shoes first, just to be sure they really work with your wardrobe in the way you want them to. Then after a day or so, you can go back and duplicate. Sometimes, however, it's fun to find a similar but not completely identical pair. Something similar in style will serve you in the same way but also might prove more versatile creating other alternative wardrobe options.

* *Just try them on!* When it comes to shoes, no two people are the same. So if you're shopping with a

friend or your sister or mom and she squeals in discomfort at a pair of shoes that you were ogling, just try them on! One woman's shoe pain could be another's shoe pleasure.

—*Be as practical as possible:* Sure, purchase one pair of wild-child six-inch heels to bring out when the limo is coming to get you. But if you know you need to be on your feet all day long, shop much harder for those ultrafeminine but super practical sexy kitten heels that you know your real life calls for.

—*Size matters:* The same shoes in different sizes look very different on different feet and legs. Some styles (budget or luxury) can look perfect and dainty in a size 6 yet lose their entire appeal in a clunky size 10.

The psychology of shoes is a complicated matter. The right pair of shoes changes the "feel" of an entire outfit. Slip into high heels with a dress or skirt and your posture changes, and it's this that makes you feel different, more confident. Heels adjust your posture and exaggerate the curve in your back, giving off a very sexy vibe.

Your posture and body psychology when you are wearing flats is completely different. Flats can make you feel very open, relaxed, and casual, just like they look. Low or kitten heels make the vaguest sexy suggestion, and subtlety is a huge part of the psychology of shoes. Being aware of this will change how you look at your shoe collection and how it matches your wardrobe. Grab a pair of shoes from your closet and as you try them on, think how they make you *feel*. It could be *cool, on fire, confident, secure, casual, artsy, fun, relaxed, in pain, insecure, dumpy,* or just *tall.* No matter what the word, you can use this vibe to help you match your shoes to your clothing. Think of it as "shoe intuition." If you really get into it, you can even label the box with a sticker (if they are stored in boxes) or underneath on the shoe if they are not just to remind you of this.

HOW TO AQUIRE FANTASY SHOES

Every girl deserves at least one pair of fantasy shoes. There are whole tribes of women out there who budget their clothes *so* carefully every season because for them; it's all about the shoes. That pair of fabuloso new shoes comes before even a brand new white tee.

Just having a pair of fantastic shoes, in the box, with the lovely smell, the soft shoe bag, and the crinkly paper, is a feel-good experience that every girl should have at least once. Whether you crave the artistry of Manolo Blahniks, Jimmy Choos, Sergio Rossis, Guccis, Pradas, or other extortionate luxury pair and whether you get them from eBay for half price, from a store brand new, from a silent auction, from someone as a gift, or from a consignment store, picking a style that you *actually wear* fre-

Style File: Closet Compromises

It's okay to have a fantasy pair of shoes, but it's not okay to go into debt getting them. If you *must* have them, cut back on something else. Recycle your coats for a season or place a self-imposed embargo on new winter boots to compensate for the splurge!

quently will enhance your enjoyment further. However, if your fantasy pick is pink, frilly, and just plain silly but you just craved them, you still deserve them as a gift to yourself.

One of the best and most satisfying ways to accomplish getting a fantasy pair of shoes is to sell something else deliberately. This way you very specifically narrow the big financial gap! Have a garage sale, send some stuff to consignment, or do some extra babysitting or dog sitting. It'll add up pretty soon if you squirrel that money away into your "shoe fund." *Call* it your shoe fund! Then, when your cash has stacked up and you see your dream pair, it won't hurt your pocketbook as much. The dream shoes will feel even more well deserved and not a guilty pleasure as if you swiped cash from the housekeeping budget to satisfy your craving.

HOW TO CARE AND STORE YOUR SHOES PROPERLY

Does your closet look like a big mess with sandal straps and boot heels all poking out from the lower regions? Are your winter and summer pairs all thrown together? If that's the case, do you realize that your options for using your prized possessions are limited? Ever heard of out of sight, out of mind? It's a bit like that with shoes. And the more shoes you have, the more you forget you have. And keeping your shoes unruly definitely gives you a fashion disadvantage.

If you're racing out somewhere and can't find what you want, you're not going to be stylistically open to other shoe choices because you just don't see them. Here's an example: Maybe you're standing in a tried and tested outfit (a pretty garden party dress), but the weather is too rainy for the strappy sandals you would normally wear with it. If your closet is neatly organized, you'll have no problem picking out a lesser-worn pair that could work great for today. For those shoes that are without boxes (flip-flops, etc.), the

Got Storage?

On any professional fashion shoot, a stylist will keep and place like-minded things together. By putting the categories of clothing and colors together, you will find it so much easier on the eye and so much easier when you reach in to select something suitable. If your wardrobe needs a reconfiguration, try reorganizing like this:

- Separate each garment by category (jackets, pants, etc.).

- Hang or organize by color (warm colors all together, graduating to cool). Note: sweaters should never be hung as they will stretch!

- Sort by style (skinny pants with skinny pants, boot cut with other boot-cut pants, etc.).

- Sort by texture (silk with silk, cotton with cotton, etc.). Sensitive fabrics should *always* be separated to prevent color bleeding. This means no mohair next to velvet for it will truly shed! Sequins or other embellished clothing should hang alone, or they can accidentally cut other items.

super-convenient fabric or vinyl storage compartments allow you to stash away, but still see, what it is you have, and that's worth tons. Coordinating everything so it can be seen at one glance is a sure way for pairs that look dated to stand out. Up close against the newer pairs, the old past-their-sell-by-date styles that need to go to the big shoe graveyard in the sky won't be so hard to part with.

Stash 'n' stack

You've probably read this in dozens of magazines, but if you haven't already, heed it now: put your shoeboxes to work for you. Snap Polaroids or print digital photos of your shoes and stick the pictures on the front of the boxes. Assuming you return your shoes to their boxes after each wear, you'll always know exactly where everything is.

A word to the wise: if your shoes are in need of repair, get thee to the cobbler, *before* you need them again. If you've stowed away your black knee-high boots for the summer without making necessary repairs, you simply won't remember that they have a tip missing when the weather gets cool again and you reach for boots. You may feel you don't want to spend repair money now, but it's a great feeling to tuck away your shoe stock, knowing it's in good condition.

How you store shoes and boots in your closet depends on the space available. Boxes stacked four or five high, either on the floor or on shelves, are not too unwieldy. If you like, each stack can represent a particular color or style. The trick is to use space in your closet that is hard to reach but still easy to see for storing off-season shoes. Keeping your off-season shoes at the top of your closet where you do not climb to very often, but where you can still see the pictures at a glance, is perfect. That way, if the weather is unseasonable, funky, and obscenely hot or cold, you can see all the options available to you. Think "Storage According to Usage." In other words, place the shoes you use the most in the most accessible place.

You've already learned that shoes stored carefully in a box stay in better condition than those tossed randomly on the closet floor, but the case for seeing what you have when you need it is more than worth the boxing up. Some very organized fashion professionals or just fashion-conscious people like to see all the same *categories* of their shoes together, so that when pumps are called for, what's available is all pumps right there in the stack. Stylists often prefer to see shoe choices by color so that when brown or neutral shoes are desired, for example, the entire range from heels to flats is all there. If you live in a four-season

Style File: Giving Your Shoes the Boot

You know which shoes are past their sell-by dates when you no longer feel they deserve a box of their own! So toss them. Sometimes you have to say good-bye to a pair of old friends, but you'll be making space for some new ones.

city, where extreme weather makes for some unpredictable shoe emergencies, you'll have to be more vigilant about keeping a variety of seasonal shoes handy.

WHAT TO SHOP IN SEPTEMBER

* Pocketbooks and wallets
* Fall/winter bags
* Winter boots
* Party dresses
* Sweaters
* Winter day dresses
* Winter separates

Pocketbooks and wallets can be bought at any time of year especially if they're classic and you aim to hang on to them forever. However, September has the best fall offerings on the shelves. A great *fall or winter bag* purchased now will carry you through an Indian summer, a prolonged or short fall, and the whole winter until the warm weather of next spring takes hold in March or April. Your new bag could be attached at your shoulder for the next eight months, so pick wisely! That said, if you've been craving a status bag or bag indulgence, buy it now.

Look, too, for the hottest *winter boots* and *party dresses* that will be bursting out of the stores right about now, so if you need to replenish and have the resources, go for it. It may not feel anything like the holiday season yet, but the dresses on the racks in the stores will allude to the coming season, so take heed! It may still be scorching outside, but the little black dress issue (and hopefully other more exciting colors) can be solved right now. If you'll likely do the rounds of holiday parties and know that you need something fresh, pick it now. Forward planning, as always, will serve you best. Winter boots hit their peak in September, although it's not necessary to buy new ones each year. If you've uncovered your boots from a past season and you can recycle them because they're classics (such a satisfying feeling), you've just saved yourself time—and money! And if your boots are still in great condition, but they're feeling rather old to you, try pairing them with your new fall pieces. Often a new dress or separates can give your older boots a new lease on life.

The fall clothing racks are brimming with new tantalizing styles such as new *sweaters, winter day dresses,* and separates such as pants, skirts, and long-sleeved tees. In terms of choices, there's a lot going on this month and your budget can only go so far. But that doesn't mean you can't pick up some great stuff. Hit the great high-fashion low-priced fashion brands in stores like JCPenney and H&M first if you need more than a few of your key wardrobe categories and you're strapped for cash.

If you're going to go for one critical purchase, splurge for the month of September before anything else and get inspired with a new pocketbook. I know stylists and trendsetters who wouldn't dream of going into a new season without a new bag. If you've already gotten your coat and boot choice in mind, naturally you'll want to finish the look off with an exterior accessory that works hard and looks great. However, if you've a pocketbook that you're absolutely in love with and you can get away with it for another season, that's fine—there's not a hard and fast rule on this.

TIPS FOR A LOWER TAB

If you're looking to add some character to your wardrobe without breaking the bank, vintage shoes are a fun item to shop for. Don't disregard them as no-life-left budget buys. If you hit lucky with sizing, you may be able to pick up a pair of vintage designer shoes at a fraction of the cost that have style, character, and collector's appeal and have barely been worn.

If you prefer new shoes, as I mentioned earlier, check the large discount shoe warehouse-style stores and outlets first. Their range of brands is astounding, and because they stock in bulk, their prices will be the best anywhere. You can also order shoes online, from either eBay or other online stores, but you can't try them on like this. However, if you know that you're a size 7 in Christian Louboutin sandals (because you already have a pair or have tried on a pair), chances are that another style in that same size will fit okay. It's good to know what size fits you perfectly in your favorite designer luxury shoes so that when you're cruising the Internet or come unexpectedly upon a clearance sale, you can go directly for the jugular—scoring a pair of discounted designer shoes is cutthroat!

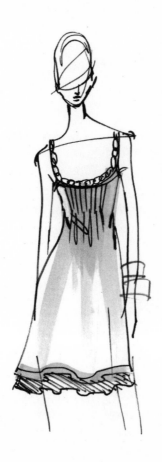

* OCTOBER *

Fashion Etiquette

I once did a fashion segment on TV called "Politically Correct Dressing." Naturally, it brought up the whole debate about what's acceptable or rather what's *politically correct* when we get dressed, and, moreover, what's politically correct *now* versus what was acceptable years ago.

Our ideas of fashion etiquette have changed drastically over the decades. Even our expectations of decency have changed. These days, showing skin is very much in. Today, anything goes! In fact, creative dressers have learned to use irony and humor when styling outfits.

As a culture we've moved through a gradual dressing down of the workplace and the concept of casual Fridays so that now casual dressing is much more of an everyday occurrence in many corporate environments. How did this happen? Well, the fashion industry may be a bit of a crazy one changing its mind every season about almost everything, but it's not an island! It just goes to show that fashion is as much a part of the mix that drives popular culture. Influences like cable TV and tabloids have definitely played a huge part in changing fashion etiquette.

Plus, age is so indeterminable today. Who can tell the age of anyone anymore. It's so much more subject to attitude and demeanor than actual wrinkles and years! Even the professionals agree! I've enlisted some top designers—real fashion insiders at the highest level—to corroborate this phenomenon.

WHAT THE HECK IS FASHION ETIQUETTE ANYWAY?

Fashion etiquette is *situational*. There's not one rule that covers all dilemmas. Fashion etiquette is dressing yourself up or down deliberately in a way that respects others. If you're in a conservative setting, etiquette dictates that you dress conservatively. Conforming to a dress code shows care for other people's sensitivities. But really just to complicate things, *everyone* in fashion seems to have different views about the nuances of fashion etiquette. So just to prove my point, I gathered some of New York's finest fashion designers and asked them for their disparate views on this majorly tricky subject: fashion etiquette and styling conundrums. As you can see, it's a cross section (and a hilarious selection) of opinions.

The posse of top New York–based designers are:

Jeff Mahshie—Creative Director (Chaiken)
Cynthia Steffe—Designer
Catherine Malandrino—French-born Designer
Marc Bouwer—Designer
Nicole Miller—Designer
Betsey Johnson—Designer
Luca Orlandi—Italian-born Designer (Luca Luca)
Traver Rains—One half of the design duo Heatherette

Q. Can you wear white after Labor Day?

BETSEY: Duh? Yeah.

LUCA: Don't forget, 90 percent of the world does not even celebrate Labor Day, so do as you please.

CYNTHIA: I love white all year round. This country's climate is so varied that white is always appropriate, no matter where you live or what the season.

CATHERINE: No rules and regulations in fashion. Style is about an open mind!

NICOLE: Yes. Everyone has heard of winter whites. Just try to stay away from pants.

MARC: Who said you can't wear white? That's rubbish!

Q: If you wear gloves or a hat at a fancy lunch, should you remove them to eat?

JEFF: Yes.

LUCA: Absolutely.

NICOLE: No. Because there is nothing worse than hat hair.

Q: Can you wear open-toe sandals with stockings?

CATHERINE: No!

CYNTHIA: Never.

NICOLE: Only wear open sandals with opaque tights.

BETSEY: Generally, I am against do's and don'ts; however, sheer stockings under sandals? It's so "unright." But kneesocks and slides? You see, that works!

TRAVER: Get a pedicure and take off the socks!

LUCA: Yes, but don't expect your man to tell you how sexy you are!

Q. Can you wear bare legs in winter?

LUCA: Yes, of course. If you are tan, even better.

CATHERINE: I love it. It's so sexy with a dress, a fur, and snow.

JEFF: Definitely, especially at night. Evening clothes have no season.

CYNTHIA: Absolutely! I especially love the look of bare legs and boots.

Q. Can you wear white as a wedding guest?

CATHERINE: Yes.

NICOLE: Bad idea. I have seen it done, but don't approve.

LUCA: Only if you hate the bride.

JEFF: Men can wear white dinner jackets. Otherwise, only if white is requested on the invitation. For women, there are so many options, it is not necessary.

CYNTHIA: This is one of those gray areas. Never wear a white dress. I've seen white suits worn at weddings, but as a rule why go there?

BETSEY: If you are sensitive to the bride, show her some classic old-fashion respect, and let her be the only one dressed in white.

Q. What would you never wear mixed together?

CATHERINE: Everything can be mixed together. My best friend wore Hermès towels wrapped around his body as a shawl for a black tie event. My husband always wears colorful sneakers with black tie and breaks it up with a Lacoste Polo.

LUCA: I would never mix my clothes with my wife's. If you want to cross-dress, do it fully!

TRAVER: The one thing that never goes with anything is a pair of flats. Boring and not sexy.

CYNTHIA: Mixing and matching is a personal thing, but I like things to have a focused look. I would never wear a turtleneck with a necklace or a turtleneck with a scarf.

MARC: Mixing is exciting. But try not to do head-to-toe matching.

BETSEY: I hate matchy-matchy. And my pet hate is a denim jacket and denim jeans.

Q: So, what is your version of fashion etiquette then?

JEFF: It's about looking appropriate for the occasion. You don't need the newest or most expensive item, you need to be appropriate.

CATHERINE: There's no fashion etiquette. It's all about personality and style.

NICOLE: Don't wear the latest trend.

LUCA: Clean clothes.

MARC: It's about knowing your personal limitations with your body type. If you're stepping out to a charity dinner and you have an enormous chest, fashion etiquette is not wearing a dress with a slit down to the navel!

TRAVER: Etiquette is important according to the circumstances. But I love it when someone shows up to work or the grocery store decked out like they are headed to a paparazzi-crazed red carpet!

BETSEY: Be yourself and suffer the consequences!

So that takes care of the old-fashion stigmas, but are there any new rules that apply to all? Not exactly, and that's great, really. You and I are all free to make our own. There's *every* reason why your own personal interpretation of what's right can—and should—be different from your best friend's or your mom's. So let's make some new guidelines that work for you!

LET'S LOOK AT YOUR
PERSONAL STYLE BAROMETER

Veteran *Vogue* editor (and great friend) Laurie Schechter is my personal style barometer whenever I get into a conundrum. Her ideas of what's okay to wear and how to tweak what you *want* to wear are smart guidelines for just about every situation. I live and swear by them, but you decide for yourself.

The solution is: when in doubt, yank 'em off!

"Visible panty lines never, ever look good," is one of Laurie's main mantras. If you're planning to wear a super-tight dress or pants, go commando. Having said that, if you're a modest mouse, replace your panties with a pair of control top pantyhose that are often nicely fitted and hug the body well, helping you feel protected, but not naked. A biker-short corseted shaper works great too, if you still prefer to wear something underneath but also want bare legs. By the way, there's nothing wrong with a very skinny thong. As long as you can't see it peeking out or through a dress or pants.

A little lingerie goes a long, long way, no matter your age!

Wear your underwear as outerwear sparingly. Very sparingly. It's okay to take your lingerie slip dresses out to the lounge or bar if you're in your twenties. But for the rest, allowing only a peek of lingerie for a look of subtle seduction is much better. For real—less is more.

The 40 percent rule

When getting dressed pick an item that makes the strongest statement (hint, it's likely to be your trendiest piece) and figure out a way to style it so that it contributes to no more than 40 percent of your total look. The idea here is to simplify your trendy looks and learn the art of moderation. It's never good to mix too many trends or go trendy head to toe. Forty percent is still a pretty flexible percentage for you to express yourself!

The use of your fashion intelligence

Roughly translated, fashion intelligence is simply thinking ahead and planning what to wear. Plus, it's all about being mindful of *where* you are. Especially if you're going somewhere you've not been before, you score points for finding out what's expected ahead of time. There's an element of fashion intelligence that feeds off being interactive with your surroundings. For example, if you're going to a job interview, it's about dressing as if you already have the job. Suppose the job is with a trendy, city-based advertising agency, some fabulous jeans, a fashion-forward jacket, and heels will be more *fashion intelligent* than a standard interview suit and pumps. Your fashion intelligence shows when you do as you're expected. You don't need to be a rebel and yell your style just because you're going somewhere out of your normal context. Just conform to your new situation; it's classier. You can go back to your mad-kick style ways when you're back on familiar ground later.

Mixes and matches

In fashion, opposites often do attract, so classic pairings aren't just a great way to make an outfit interesting, but they can be a unique expression of your personal style. Tweeds and pearls can look matronly if they're styled in a grandma way (below the knee and worn with one classic one string of pearls). But add a tweed jacket to a super-sized choker of pearls, tight jeans, and heels, and the whole effect completely changes. Only you can judge the fashion barometer of whether certain elements or opposites are in at any given time, and thus how ironic they look paired together. PS: You want to aim for some irony occasionally when you're getting dressed. It's a sophisticated element of style.

For example, if you have diamonds, it's interesting to see them worn in a less glamorous setting than with evening-wear. Jeans, a tee, and high heels are a fun pairing with diamonds. The irony comes from the fact that jeans are normally worn in a casual way. But this way, it's a perfect way to take denim from day to night.

Specific textiles like leather and lace tend to be in or out of style at any given time. Again, leather and lace are opposites—leather is tough and lace is softer, more romantic. So tough masculine biker-style leather pants and flat biker boots take on a feminine theme when a peek of lace is seen popping out of your top half, be it from under a sweater, cardigan, or whatever. If you are aiming to develop style icon status, leather is probably a regular part of your fashion vocabulary in the form of something in a classic shape that lasts forever (like leather pants).

Strangely enough, there's no such thing as total "ick factor" in fashion. In other words, odd pairings, oddly, can look great. But that doesn't mean you can throw all caution to the wind. It's wise to avoid certain silhouettes that are unflattering on some body types. Short people don't look great in very long coats or pieces with lots and lots of fabric, for example. A big ruffled balloon dress with tiers and bold colors can look ridiculous on someone less than statuesque or Amazonian. So know your Rx for balancing your personal shape. If you can't figure it out from dressing and undressing at home, head to your nearest department store and enlist the (free) services of a personal shopper to help you decide what not to wear.

WHAT TO SHOP IN OCTOBER

* Holiday outfits
* Parkas
* Party shoes
* Belts
* Costume jewelry

Though the August and September "rush" is over, there's still an amazing array of products in the stores this month. The seemingly never ending stocks of winter basics such as skirts, sweaters, and denim are still around. But if you've already gotten your fill of these, I say go browse around for *holiday outfits,* warm *parkas, party shoes,* and the first *gift items* that will appear now.

The holiday outfits may include separates like *sweaters,* which will do double duty long after this holiday season (often there are metallics that are great neutrals the rest of the year). There will also be holiday dresses or dresses with the Christmassy or New Year's appeal of sequins or other shimmery embellishments. Dressy blouses can appear now too. These are for wearing as "separates" to pair with dressy pants or skirts as an alternative to the dress option. Season-less skirts are always useful. So you might see something classic and lightweight like a pencil skirt or maybe something in denim. October is a versatile month in terms of weather, which means that any seasonless purchases made now can be worn right now, very gratifyingly. If you pick these up now, you will find you can wear them well into next year.

If you've spent heavily in September, you may want to limit your October retail therapy to a few updating accessories like *belts* or *costume jewelry*. These accessories can be bought all year, but it's amazing how your new flats or boots (bought in August or September) paired with your new bag (from September) is transformed by an up-to-date necklace, a new watch, or a new belt. Belts are a great expression of individual style for winter, especially a very cold winter! When it's below zero out and you feel converted to jeans, corduroys, and turtlenecks for the foreseeable future, investing in a belt can truly personalize and dress up your outfit. As my pal jewelry stylist Annalee Lucas puts it, a new belt at this time of year is fabulous "winter bling." And you can tie in an outrageous belt with earrings, also, to ensure a demure balance since these pieces aren't worn close together.

If you see a minxy little party dress in October, get it now, and it'll be your "party staple" for months to come. Even if you don't regularly attend many events, the party dresses available this month are the best of the bunch. With seasonless dressing so popular, nothing you get now will just be for the cooler weather. Ditto for the party shoes. Right now they can be fabulous. Pick out festive shoes in metallics and those embellished with jewels while the selection is good. They'll carry over to other seasons.

Warm parkas, casual, funky, or smart, are great jackets for

the in-between weather. They're obviously not a cover-all for full-on snowstorms, but they're great for windy fall days and as alternatives to full-length coats for casual dressing. Parka styles do change each year, so if you want a trendy jacket, just remember that it may have to sit out a season or two after you've worn it through one winter. If you're a ski bunny, you'll be hotly anticipating the upcoming snow season. The first of the new *ski outfits* will arrive in specialty stores around the end of October or early November, so it's a great moment (before you set off to the mountains) to check out what's in the stores. The shops at the ski resort will have the latest styles, but if you plan to take your ski trip in February or March, there'll be much less stock to choose from than what's in the stores right now.

Tips for a Lower Tab

The hardware on a warm parka is a dead giveaway for spotting true luxury or trendiness. The high-end luxury parkas have fastenings, buttons, closures, or toggles that are heavy and well made and hardware-like zippers that are substantial. They also have beautiful linings and often real fur trim. To save, pick faux fur instead, but be careful not to pick a skimpy zipper or cheap-looking closures.

Unless you are a diehard ski bunny and intend to spend weeks on end in the mountains, the importance of the newest styles in skiwear may not be *so* critical to you. In which case, you can scour eBay, but I say, only for unworn product. If something is worn, you want to see in person how worn and where. If you actually have time to check out if there is a thrift store in the ski town or resort that you will visit (search for them ahead of your trip online), you can sometimes get the most amazing "seconds." I have been to the thrift store called Soosies in Aspen, Colorado, and there are some luxury pieces for great prices. Just try them on! You will already be wrapped in warm sweaters and layers and should be able to tell how well things fit and how warm they will be. Check, too, the sale rack within the skiwear-dedicated store for last year's styles—they're new and unworn!

The Red-Carpet Rules

Boy, have things changed. Not unlike wedding-guest dressing, formalwear has become much more casual in recent years. The styling options for dressing for a big event or party are more flexible than ever. But if you always come unstuck when you receive a formal party invite, you should adopt a formula that will always help you get it right. This could include interpreting the invite, styling yourself in conjunction with your date, or listening to how you feel that day.

Moreover, be flexible and open-minded about changing what you plan to wear. Haven't you ever heard a celebrity on the red carpet say, "Well, I was planning to wear such-and-such. But then, this afternoon, I just slipped into this dress that my stylist brought over, and it just *felt* so good!" Well, that's exactly how it can happen for you at home. What works in your mind's eye when you're planning to get dressed for an upcoming party might not feel quite right or as good on the night of the event. This can *even* happen when you have taken the trouble to go out and buy something special for a specific occasion, but that's okay. If this happens, give yourself a break. The key is to be sure you look and feel your most glamorous because after all that's what red-carpet dressing is all about. You may not have an actual red carpet to walk down, but formals and formal dressing occasions come up no less in our noncelebrity lives.

INVITATION INTERPRETATION

In these days of e-mail and text messages, it feels like such a luxury to get an actual invitation in the mail, on good card stock, all made out nicely to you the guest. Thankfully, formal occasions still warrant a fancy invitation that you can actually hold in your hand. The information printed on this swanky piece of stationery will give you all the details about the party, and that should include the dress code. However, if you receive an invitation to an event or party and there is no dress code specified, you can use your fashion intelligence to read between the lines.

Here are my three guidelines:

1. **Rank the party *invitation and location* on a scale of 1 to 5 on poshness!** Is this a posh party? A party to dress up for? A true celebration? How formal is it? Is the invitation an evite, or did it come in the mail on gorgeous cream-colored card stock with a gold edging?

   Rank the party by invitation and location, with 1 being a casual after-work drinks thing and 5 being a wedding gala in a city hotel.

2. **Rank the *time of day* on a scale of 1 to 5 for formality**, with 1 being breakfast and 5 being dinner and dancing. Think about the time of day of the party or event. Is it lunch, tea, dinner, drinks, or later than dinner? Generally, the later in the day, the more formal the event. Rank the party by time of day, with

1 being breakfast or brunch and 5 being dinner and dancing.

3. **Rank the *relationship* you have to the person or group involved.** This should not necessarily be how well you know the person, it should also take into account the formality or professional nature of the relationship. If it is very formal or professional (like your boss), it should rank as a 5 and the most comfortable and cozy relationship (like your sister) as a 1.

Now add your scores together.

1 to 5—casual

Your event is casual. Possibly during the daytime, with family or very close friends. A backyard barbecue at your sister's on a Saturday at lunchtime, for example, is a classic 1–5 type event. The weekend daytime hour, your warm and fuzzy relationship with your sister, and the event taking place outside, all keep the ranking low. Shorts, Capris, jeans, tees, even flip-flops, or a sundress may be the way to go here. Other casual events may call for jeans and tees or a simple dress and boots if it's a work-related invite or seasonally cool.

6 to 10—cocktail chic

Your event is likely to be in the middle of the dress-up scale. Perhaps the invite is for a dinner at a fancy restaurant to celebrate your best friend's engagement. The fact that it's your best friend's party keeps the dress code groovy and casual, but the fancy restaurant and evening hour pushes the rank up. A flowy cocktail dress, a trendy skirt and sexy top, or a trendy pantsuit with heels may be the way to go here.

11 to 15—formal

Okay, you're obviously heading for an event near or at the top of the dress-up scale. Perhaps attending a special dinner honoring someone or attending a special evening with your boss, your husband, and their colleagues will call for special attire. Luckily, for such an event there might even be an actual *physical* invite that states the dress code. If not, it's going to be up to you to judge how sexy your dress should be, how much skin to cover up, how long or short a dress to wear, and how much carefully calibrated bling you add on!

DRESS CODE DECODER

Hasn't everyone received an invitation to a party with a dress code that needs decoding? If you are flummoxed by what to wear when a party invite reads "Black Tie Optional" or "Dress Festive," you're not the only one! There's no need to panic though. Here's the key to every dress code you could imagine!

Casual dress

Casual is casual, so if it's summer, then shorts and a tank top will probably work fine. However, be smart about the venue. A party or a clambake on a beach calls for shorts and tank top; if it's an invite to a BBQ at someone's home, a sundress might be a better choice. For any time of the year other than midsummer (when they will just be too hot), jeans are the answer here.

Smart casual

When a host writes "Smart Casual," she is essentially hand-ing you a peace offering! He or she wants you to be com-fortable but also wants guests dressed up a little so that the event feels special. Depending on the weather, you can cer-tainly wear casual dress (like the outfit you'd select for the previous category) ramped up with accessories. Switch to heels instead of flats and a smarter pocketbook, perhaps. Jeans are still totally cool as long as you dress them up.

Business casual

You get the green light to drop the formality of a business situation here. *But not totally.* The key to the perfect busi-ness casual outfit is to avoid wearing a suit, and instead wear mixed pieces that give the silhouette of one. A suit jacket with a loose cute top underneath is a perfect exam-ple. If you stick to a structured outfit, you won't feel inap-propriate. Sometimes it depends on where you're planning to wear biz casual. If it's the more relaxed West Coast, a groovy shirt and pants works fine. On the East Coast, a tai-lored dress might be more appropriate. The key is not to go too trendy, and if you have to wear denim, make sure it's elegant denim. If you don't think you can pull off a refined denim look (it's very tricky to get right), say no to denim. Period!

Dress creative

Anytime I've seen "Dress Creative," I always think the invite is begging its recipients to dress more fun! It's about getting dressed up for fun rather than formality. It could mean that you incorporate something retro or pick a vintage look or something that's fun to dance in. Think adventurously; think about being noticed. The beauty of this one is that it's truly up to your own imagination how far you go.

Dress festive

This is fun, not scary. Festive dress means your host wants everyone to mingle together. Depending on the holiday, be it Christmastime, Thanksgiving, or Fourth of July, it's a license (and an excuse) to dress sexier or fancier than you might normally. If the occasion is a cocktail hour, you might wear a slightly longer dress than a short one. Or add an extra accessory that amps up the festive look for night. Take care not to be too theme driven.

Dinner jacket required

Once in a while, this men's dress code will be found posted at certain restaurants, often quite unexpectedly. Even then, these outdated words can be confusing with a different interpretation for each establishment. They can mean *you need to* wear a tie or *a tie is not necessary, but a jacket is.* Sometimes it means something completely different, like *no sneakers* (a helluva way of saving so). If you know that dinner jackets are required at a venue, be sure your date or husband wears a great shirt that can be worn with or without a tie. Make sure, too, that the jacket complements both the slacks and the shirt. For a woman it's only appropriate that the look is more refined when dinner jackets are required.

Cocktail attire

Oh, cocktail parties! Drinking cocktails and cocktail dresses by their very nature are fun. Pick a dress that is short to the knee but not so short that you look like you are off to a nightclub. A conservative skirt suit or narrow cigarette pants or dressed-up pantsuit in this style can be dressy enough too, but a cocktail dress trumps a suit every time! And a cocktail dress gives you an opportunity to show a little sparkle and add some blingy jewelry. The only key to remember here is not to wear a long dress to a cocktail party as you will look and feel overdressed.

Creative black tie

Creative black tie is an unusual option. It's the trendy way to wear black tie. It's a license to drop the conservative confines of traditional black tie and have some fun. For men it can mean something like a velvet tux worn with jeans, and for women a fun retro cocktail dress. One great interpretation is a standard tux or dress paired with over-the-top accessories. Maybe a cravat for a man and chunky costume jewels for a woman. Either way, creative black tie is more tongue in cheek than traditional black tie, so use black tie as your foundation, and build on it with your own expression of style. But stop shy of looking costumey.

Black tie optional

In essence, this dress code gives you a choice. If you don't want to don your tux or wear a long gown, you need not. Obviously, the event or party is a formal occasion, so even if you don't show up in black tie, dress smartly for the occasion. For men, choose a suit and tie rather than mixed slacks and a jacket. For women, a very fancy skirt is okay.

Better still, pick a dress. However, even though it might be inconvenient, if your host has specified the party as black tie optional, donning your finest eveningwear is the way to go. Figure out a way to make it happen!

Black tie

A black-tie event translates into two words: classy party. It is imperative that you dress accordingly. Short or long cocktail dresses or gowns fitted or flowing are fine. Personally, I prefer to wear a shorter dress with no train trailing after me unless I am attending a party with a date. When I go it alone, I can generally navigate the party better in a shorter zippier number, but that is just a totally personal choice. If you wear a long dress when you arrive to a black-tie

Style File: Coat Check

For a formal occasion, don't wear your regular coat. A shawl, wrap, fur, stole, or sparkly evening coat are all perfect and elegant for black tie.

event with a man, he can feel like a gent as he has the job of watching your step for you. He will anticipate your needs as you get in and out of the car, and, hopefully, he will fetch you a drink and generally look after you if you are in an impossibly beautiful dress (especially one with a train). You can vaguely live out the vulnerable damsel-in-distress fantasy here!

White tie

White tie is a very special state of dress, evoking an era gone by and older traditions. If you plan to attend white tie, find, beg, borrow, or steal a breathtaking gown, which really should be long and have a stunning train. You can go all the way with accessories too. Long gloves are so elegant and really finish the look here, but be sure you remove them to eat! You can wear your cocktail rings and bracelets over long gloves, it's a very stylized look, or only wear gloves for making an entrance. If the weather is cold, do wear a stunning fur or cape, even if you have to beg, borrow, or buy one. High-wattage jewels fit white tie the best, and even a discreet tiara works if you have one or can borrow one. Your date should wear not only a white or silver tie and wing collars but also an accompanying vest and longer coattails (sometimes known as morning dress) in place of a regular tux. This is *evening-time* fairytale dressing, pure and simple.

Morning dress

Morning dress is the daytime equivalent of white tie. It's the kind of dress worn to events taking place before 5 p.m. For you, a truly elegant suit, hat and gloves, or elegant knee dress and coat combination works. Your date really gets the treatment here. The morning coat is long and gray or black and paired with a waistcoat. The formal pants are gray and striped, and an ascot tie looks great with a French cuff stiff shirt and stiff white collar. Suspenders prevent his waistband from appearing below the waistcoat. And to top it all off, a black silk or gray top hat and formal gloves in kid leather finish this dapper look off! Morning dress is rare, but some daytime weddings, state events in some European countries, and, of course, very fancy horse racing events do demand it. This is *daytime* fairytale dressing.

State dress

Okay, if you are going to meet a king, queen, or head of state at a formal evening gala (not at a polo match or horse race), you are going to need to research what is expected at the event in question. Military service uniforms are usually required for service members (both men and women). For everyone else, you should ask in great detail what is expected of the dress code when you RSVP. You do not want to get this one wrong! State dress is a potential fashion etiquette minefield. Certain occasions, for example, might or might not require hats or other head coverings, sashes that coordinate with your date, and gloves or no gloves. It will entirely depend on the event. Do find out *exactly* what is expected for any kind of military, state, or royal events by contacting whoever invited you.

YOUR OWN RED-CARPET STYLE

So you're going to a dressed-up affair. Hopefully, you have a few party dresses as options in your closet, but what do you feel like wearing tonight? Just because you love your long black dramatic goth lace dress that always gets lots of compliments doesn't mean you feel it tonight. Dressing to suit how you *feel* is an often underestimated and valuable asset to your personal style. It's not so much about finding a style that's *always* you, but more about dressing according to your style mood on the day of the event. See if you relate to any of these roles.

The Minimalist

Think Gwyneth Paltrow. Minimal means minimal with the dress and all the accessories—even the hair. How does it feel to dress as the Minimalist? You feel cool, serene, clear-headed, calm, and controlled. So, if you want to have that kind of evening, maybe you have a dress in your closet that's unfussy with clean lines that isn't too tight or itchy or hasn't any embellishment at all. For the hair, try either up in a tight strict chignon or down and pancake flat close to your head. Discreet understated jewelry fits this look and makes it more starkly beautiful. If you're very brave, you can even try out your most glamorous flats instead of heels to give your entire posture and stature a simplicity that everyone else will lack (because they'll be wearing heels). Your image will pervade if you wear a knowing enigmatic smile with this outfit. It's a great look to go for if your life and your closet are just feeling cluttered, and you feel you need some space from it all!

The Natural

Think Jennifer Aniston all the way. She's never over-whelmed by her clothes, even on the red carpet. In fact, Jennifer's hair and makeup remain the same whether she's on the beach in shorts or at the Oscars in an evening gown. Her jewelry is never overwhelming either. Her natural look is just as hard to achieve as any other, but it certainly doesn't mean "do nothing!" It's a level of style subtlety that allows her personality to shine through and her face, hair, and dress take a backseat. The Natural shines best in mono-chromatic dramatic colors that work as a canvas for the face, neckline, back, and hair. These include navy, black, and brown. The focus is on the Natural, and she's never overshadowed by her dress. Go for neutral makeup, too, like pink nails and toes and soft tones on the face. Bronzer is the Natural's best friend.

The Vamp

Christina Aguilera is always a vamp. She's truly the high-holy diva of the red carpet, and her look is typified by highly stylized hair, and most importantly full-beam makeup. Overtly sexy dresses are the hallmark of the Vamp look, which oozes with dynamite sex appeal. To pull off the full effect of the Vamp, you need to be in a mood that says, "Look at me, I'm strong and dangerous." You need to be in the mood to strut in your lowest-cut sexiest dress, your most teetering high heels, and your full quota of bling bling. The red vampy nails and lipstick will give you a style edge, but don't go over the top and don't dazzle or sparkle from every pore. Tone it down when you're done by removing one bold feature, such as your earrings or nail polish. And do take that careful last look in the mirror just to keep it real. Don't jump over the line from vamp to drag queen!

The Lady

Reese Witherspoon is the ultimate Lady. Her looks are always classic, decorous, and polished. Poise is the word you want to keep in mind here. Your stable of little black dresses (and even a long black dress) should be a good guideline for getting your style antenna tuned in to the ways of the Lady. But this is not an excuse to go for a black dress that is safe but boring. The Lady dresses impeccably with a hint of sexiness—never risqué. Classic column gowns in solid colors, prints, or especially metallics are her signature. But A-line cocktail dresses àla 1940s fit here too.

Shoes can be flirty and very high, and hair can be up or down and classic or contemporary in style. The makeup, whether old school or modern, is feminine but never edgy. Marilyn Monroe's red lips work great here, but that kind of feminine statement is always worn in accordance with the rest of her look. So, if you do the big red scarlet lip thing, go nude or barely there on the eyes, or vice versa. The mood you are creating when you dress as the Lady is a flirty "come hither" but with very proper intentions and manners to boot!

The x factor

Next you should always create some extra room to consider the dreaded x factor. The *x* factor will screw up your plans and make you reconsider your options. You might well have thought out a perfect outfit or a dress for this event but:

* It's pouring rain out
* You have PMS and feel fat in *that* dress

If this happens, don't be hard on yourself, there's nothing wrong with changing outfits late in the game. You reserve the right to change your mind according to your mood. Trying to put a square peg in a round hole (or putting on a bright pink dress when you just feel like wearing simply black and white) won't help the experience or enjoyment of dressing up and going out. Fashion choices should make you happy not disgruntled!

STYLE YOUR DATE

Don't' tell me: you're the stylish diva of your family, always so careful to be appropriately dressed and are constantly on the receiving end of everyone's compliments, except for your boyfriend, fiancé, husband, partner, partner in fashion crime, or whatever you want to call him. He totally lets you down. Like—all the time. No, *worse,* doesn't just let you down, he *embarrasses* you with his fashion-scary ensembles. You know the drill—white socks with a dark suit, color-clashing slacks and sport coat, and the wrong, wrong, all wrong ensemble when it comes to the crucial night out in a tux. Be comforted, you're not alone! Many a stylish woman has had to remake her man to upgrade her own image.

When it comes to fashion policing your date, you can steer him away from major slipups. As West Coast–based Image Consultant and author of *Cary Grant: A Celebration of Style* (New York: Bullfinch, 2006), Richard Torregrossa is the ultimate guy's guy when it comes to men's style, and his trained eye will help you deal with your drastically dressed date:

Style File: Hollywood Hints

Watch any of the entertainment and gossip shows for hints on how celebrity couples style themselves so that you can copy their looks. Usually couples are casually but not glaringly coordinated.

Man rules

* ***Choose socks that are a closer match to the shoes, not the pants.*** Socks should be a shade darker than the pants but not as dark as the shoes, and as Richard says, "They should *only* perform an elegant transition between shoes and pants." And remember: no white socks with a suit—ever!

* *Encourage your man to be a gentleman* at a formal
  event by suggesting he play the romantic role. His goal
  must be to appear as an unobtrusive background for
  you as the female companion. Why? To better show
  you off, of course! He plays it down, and you play it
  up. Opposites look fabulous together. In other words,
  his simple, monochromatic look sets off the high-
  decibel glitz that you're going for. Period.

* *Make him own his style.* Even Cary Grant did this.
  Grant loved the style of Noel Coward, especially the
  cut of his tux and the facings of the lapels. In fact, he
  emulated this style, but he first infused it with a more
  masculine edge making it his own. NB: Noel was a
  completely different body type, and Cary's ultimate signature tux style looked nothing like Noel's.

* *Contrast is more striking and stylish than similarity.* No
  matter how much he wants to, *don't* let your man be
  vulgar and copy the colors in your outfit. Matching colors
  scream "prom night." Instead, have him pick a complementary color. For example, if you're in a blue dress, a
  complementary color might be orange. If orange sounds
  difficult for a man to wear, pick out a classic suit and use
  a small orange accent such as a fabulous orange Hermès
  tie. This'll look stunning next to a woman wearing a blue
  dress. And likewise, if you wear patterns, be sure he
  sticks to solids, and vice versa. Contrast is usually more
  interesting than cloning. Other complementary colors are
  red and green, and purple and yellow. However, don't
  let the word "complementary" confuse you. These are
  simply colors that have great contrast with each other
  and so make each other stand out.

* *Teach him a thing or two about his body type.* If he's
  a heavyset man, a one-button blazer or jacket is more

slimming than a three-button. Also, show him that he has a choice of a *center vent, double vent,* or *no vent* at the back of his jacket. Different styles of jackets fit different bodies. When a man sits in a sport coat that doesn't fit well, it will bunch up. So when trying one on, he should take the time to sit in it as a test. A sport coat that fits well will fall very differently from one that does not.

* *Look to the past* when next you cuddle up to watch an old movie on the couch with your man. Maybe he will be inspired to take a few style hints from the classic movie stars. Men were dapper in the old movies, so watch the way the men carefully cross their legs. It might seem a bit prissy today, but it was to preserve the crease in their pants and not wear them out in any particular spot. (Maybe some old-fashioned manners will rub off on him too, or he will sport a dapper hankerchief afterward!)

* *Try to get him to plan ahead.* If you've an opportunity to pull out what you'll be wearing, do so. Show it to him! If you don't, bring it up in conversation and let him know what you have in mind to wear for yourself. Hopefully, this will pique his interest and lead to a conversation about what *he* should wear. If he's unsure, offer to help him choose his outfit.

Having a problem making him see the point in all this? Let him get dressed how he *thinks* he should look, and then force him in front of a *full-length mirror.* An incredibly well-kept secret is that men have not yet discovered the full-length mirror. Imagine! They work the gel in the hair, put on the shirt, and adjust the tie all in the bathroom mirror. Next, they move to the bedroom, pull on slacks, and slip on shoes that feel comfy, and then they walk away. Show your man the big picture! If he has made a fashion faux pas, he will likely be horrified when he sees the full image. Then you only have to guide and direct him to the correct course of clothing. The full-length mirror (as most women know) teaches us a lot about the entire drape of a garment as well as a clue about how things look from the waist down and front and back too.

And finally, here are my fifteen fail-safe "Red-Hot Red-Carpet Rules" for looking stylish and stunning. You go and knock 'em dead!

1. **Less is more.** Think *understatement* and you will likely arrive at a great compromise. Formal attire is by its very nature dressy and attention grabbing. Carry the smallest purse that you can find to go with your ensemble, or if you can, carry no purse at all if your date will stash your lipstick and keys in his pockets. Keep your eye on the prize, which always goes for most glamorous, not garish.

2. **Get the right shoes.** Be careful of clunky shoes. They're edgy but very often a borderline mistake. And make sure you can last a whole evening in them. If they're super high and indescribably uncomfortable, you'll feel like kicking them off halfway through the evening. Needless to say, this is a huge fashion *don't*. So please, pick some shoes you can stand to be in all night!

3. **Leave enough time to travel calmly to your destination.** Maybe this is not fashion advice *directly,* but a rushed journey can ruin your outfit. Rain or puddles can ruin hair and dress hems, and unnecessary haste can lead to fashion disasters like broken heels, crushed dresses, and broken nails. Travel by car service (or limo if you

can afford it for one night!) so that you don't stress about parking close or walking far in a gown and heels.

4. **Keep your smile on.** Maintain posture and poise at all times. Smile the *whole* evening, even if something irks you. You really will look so much more poised and beautiful. When celebrities are on show in public for a glamorous event, they act professionally even if they're having personal troubles. Check your worries at the door and enjoy your night out. Stand tall and stand still. Strike a pose. Don't be self-conscious. Don't fiddle or fidget or play with your hair, fingernails, dress, earrings, underwear, watch, pocketbook, or anything! To create an aura of glamour, you have to soak up the attention elegantly and graciously that people are giving you.

5. **Remove your sunglasses.** Always remove your sunglasses if there are cameras around. *Always.* Whether you are outside with the sun beating down or inside hiding behind them, your sunglasses really will look silly when you see the photos later. You can push sunglasses up on your head if you are being photographed at an outside event, but remove them completely before any photos are taken if you change venues and step inside.

6. **Watch out for a visible panty line.** There is really nothing as unappealing as a gorgeous woman in a slinky dress or a tight gown with her panty line showing. Twist around in front of the mirror to check from all angles. If you think you can see your panty line at some angles take action! Try on a different, potentially less visible pair; wear hosiery instead; or better still, wear nothing at all.

7. **Limit the bling.** Once you've put on all your jewelry, take one piece off. There's no point going out looking like a newly adorned Christmas tree. Too much jewelry looks very overdone. It can also distract from the elegant features of a dress and make your otherwise classy balanced look appear cheap. Less is more when adding jewelry, especially to eveningwear. Just try it on and take it off again—if necessary.

8. **Watch your watch size.** If you don't have a tiny, elegant suitable evening watch, don't wear a watch. Period! It's overfussy and overkill, so keep it simple or you can easily skip it. On a glamour-filled evening, you don't really need to know the time. If you feel the need to carry your cell phone in your tiny purse, it'll tell you the time.

9. **Use Hollywood tape.** This double-sided magic stuff sticks and sticks and sticks. It's the greatest insurance policy against a wardrobe malfunction! If you'll be dancing at a formal event, use it also to stick your feet to your shoes to help keep them on!

10. **Do not chew gum.** *Period!* You will ruin your image. If you must have something, stash a small handful of your favorite flavored Altoids as a breath checker.

11. **Use long-lasting cosmetics.** Before you apply your makeup, use a "primer" under your base. This stuff really helps your base stay on longer. The same goes for a lipstick sealant and waterproof mascara to really keep your red-carpet eyes and lips perfectly primped.

12. **Get groomed in advance, not at the last minute.** Give yourself (or go get) a full manicure and pedicure preferably the day before the big event. You don't want to be getting dressed with wet nails or only partly dried

toes. And the other two words: *hair removal*. Shave, depilate, or wax. Whatever your chosen method, just get it done. Do this two days before the big event to allow any skin irritations to subside. (Hey, no one said red-carpet glamour was a breeze!)

13. **Choose a dress in a solid color.** Stay away from prints. This hint comes from designer Catherine Malandrino. So simple, and so true!

14. **Skip any unnecessary outerwear.** Unless it's snowing out and you have something fabulous and dramatic like a cape or fur, skip the coat. If you must, opt for a light shawl or wrap. Regular outerwear or coats will simply cover and crush your gorgeous gown. PS: This is another reason to arrive and leave by limo or taxi.

15. **Do the Polaroid test.** Designer Cynthia Steffe taught me this one. When you're completely ready, take a Polaroid or snap with a digital camera. It's the best way to test your makeup, to see whether your dress is too sheer for flashbulbs and to catch the ubiquitous panty line. A picture will tell you a lot about what you shouldn't wear or do. The camera doesn't lie!

WHAT TO SHOP IN NOVEMBER

∗ Seasonless separates
∗ Holiday gift sets
∗ Shearling jackets
∗ Lingerie and pajamas

In November some great *seasonless separates* join the fall and winter staples on the racks. Then, of course, late in the month the gifts and *gift sets* arrive for the Christmas season.

There will also be *shearlings* and faux shearling jackets and *lingerie* and *pajamas* arriving in department stores.

Separates that work for all seasons are useful if you purchase only what you know will add options to your current winter wardrobe without distinct trend-led influences. You want these pieces to be anonymous so that you can make them work through next spring too. So go get these if you're still navigating the retail floors for pieces to add to your winter staples. If you specifically need a winter suit, the options will be good now, and it's a good time to invest.

But who wouldn't like to get their gift shopping out of the way before the stores become a madhouse? Fashion gifts are the greatest and some of the most flexible to return if the recipient doesn't love what you pick. Flick forward to December's gift-giving guide to make sure you get every ounce of inspiration and energy up for what can only be described as a sport—before the crush!

Lastly, if warm pajamas appeal, the warmest, fuzziest, flannel, brushed cotton, and thermal PJs are in the stores. Everyone should have a fresh pair every year. For me, thermal PJs serve as winter sweats, so I get the cutest pair I can lay my hands on, knowing I will spend a lot of time cozying up in them.

TIPS FOR A LOWER TAB

Of course, we can't talk about shopping in November and ignore the huge Black Friday or post–Thanksgiving Day sales. Black Friday is the biggest shopping day of the year, and there can be some special deals—and not just on leftovers. I'm referring to special gift sets and other fashion items specially packaged at this time of year that you intend to give as gifts for the holidays. Stores use holiday dates to encourage us to shop. If you have time off from work and can face fighting the crowds (although I'll be honest, I can't and don't) on these days, go ahead, there'll be some bargains.

Keeping the spending down in November can be hard. By now, you know whether your winter wardrobe has worked out well and whether you've had enough new choices each day to satisfy your fashion appetite. But what happens if you see a similar but *slightly* different version of a sweater or skirt you already own? Be honest and strict with yourself, and *only* buy more when you've already experienced a gap in your wardrobe or when you've worn a particular item practically to death.

Holiday Style and Gift Giving

The holiday season is party time with your family and your friends! So there are a variety of festive situations and special locations you'll have to get ready for. But beware of falling into a seasonal trap and grabbing for the same little black dress with sparkly accessories every time you go to a party. Don't get me wrong, the little black dress is a good solid standby and there's technically nothing wrong with this look, but why not change things up a bit? After all, the holidays are a time to feel extra special.

CREATE AN INDIVIDUAL HOLIDAY STYLE

It is time to get thinking about holiday parties. Who'll be there? Who are you *really* dressing for—to impress the otherwise repressed office colleagues, to dazzle a potential employer, or to flirt maybe with the cute guy across the room? In order to answer these smaller questions, you'll first need to answer a larger one: How do you really feel at the holidays? (Hint hint: we should all acknowledge that they could be stressful.) But despite the stress you may be feeling, getting dressed for the holidays should be fun and light. If you want to break out of your little black dress run and approach your holiday style from a different angle, try some of these tricks and see how your outlook and enjoyment of dressing for holiday entertainment changes:

* If you normally wear heels for holiday parties where you'll be dancing all night, why not try to create a different, more adventurous style around your party clothes with a pair of elegant flats?

* If you normally accent your monochromatic outfits with gold or silver accessories, try a different festive color like red or plum instead.

* If you've been in the stores, you know that sequined outfits abound at the holidays. And while there's no harm in adding a bit of sparkle to your outfit, if you're amping up the wattage of your holiday outfits, make sure the sequins cover an area of your body that can withstand scrutiny as sequins are certain to draw attention!

* If possible, don't show too much skin. Holiday dressing that looks too naked is trying too hard!

* If you never wear skirts or dresses, be brave and search for a simple wrap dress or skirt. Surprise your family by wearing it over the holidays, and you will create a stir.

* If you can, stay away from themey holiday apparel. You really, *really* don't need that sweater that says "Jolly Holly." If you just can't get through the season without a piece of holiday kitsch, buy some quirky reindeer pajamas and enjoy them by wearing them to bed.

* If you usually have family gatherings, why not revisit a favorite vintage piece and designate it solely for the holiday season. Wear it only at this time of year, and it will create a warm and fuzzy heirloom feeling! Maybe it's a pocketbook, jewelry, or a classic item like an Hermès scarf. Every Christmas Eve, my cousin Lilian wore an exquisitely pale green beaded floor-length cotton tunic with a pair of suede moccasins (more like smoking slippers) to host her holiday party. The party was a big one, for over one hundred people, and she wanted to be supremely comfortable but exotic and casual. This unconventional attire made her guests feel at ease, even though most of them showed up in Valentino and Chanel!

* If you're not a fan already or have never explored it fully, check out something in fur. Fur is wintry, festive, warm, and decadent. Use it for an accent, but unless you're lucky enough to own a full-length fur or shearling, don't do it head to toe or you'll look like a bear trapper. For anyone against the real thing, faux is just fine and very fabulous too.

It's the time of year for creating lists. Guest lists, shopping lists, party-planning lists, decorating lists, and so on. So why not create a style list for yourself? How about a Wish List of fashionable gifts that you'd like, whether or not you plan to buy them for yourself or perhaps receive them from your family and friends? Pin it to the refrigerator. Let anyone who is in your life know that you are planning a "makeover" of your closet, and these are just some holes that need to be filled. Make out as if it's your "aspiration" list. Use the list as a guideline to treat yourself when you accomplish (1) doing that long forgotten project, (2) clearing out the attic, (3) holding that long overdue garage sale (and so on). Your nearest and dearest will soon catch on. Grown-up kids, spouses, and even best friends will get drift of the list and will hopefully take the hint—fingers crossed!

THE STYLISH GIFT LIST

Fashion gifts are some of the most difficult to buy but are also some of the most rewarding to receive (but only when you hit on the right thing). Think about jewelry. It is one of life's most sentimental pleasures, a very necessary accessory, and the kind of fashion item that is gifted most frequently. There is a skill to giving, though, and it's not all about the amount of money you spend. If you have lots and lots of friends and family and even extended family, you might need to be even more creative to make the most of your budget. Needless to say, top designers and other people working in the fashion industry have fashion-gifting conundrums too. They solve them in various (and creative) ways.

Play the "same" game

Even though she throws in something funny and personal like a card and photo, Betsey Johnson "clones out" for holiday gifting. "Each year I figure out a really neat conservative, useful, logical, timeless gift like a cardigan and give it to everyone."

New York party girl Tinsley Mortimer, who has designed bags for the Samantha Thavasa line uses the same method. "I like to give everyone the same present, like a cute clutch. It's really good as no one gets jealous or feels that another person has a cuter gift," she says.

One-note shopping for a buyer with a long list is a brilliant solution to your gift-giving conundrums. It really pleases everyone and saves you a huge amount of time at a very busy time of year. Still unsure? Check the list of suggestions I have provided, and see how many things could be a one-note solution item. More than you think!

Betsey Johnson's favorite stocking stuffer staples are lint rollers—quite possibly the world's most useful fashion gift. "I give luggage tags too," she says. "They can be very fashionable." Catherine Malandrino offers up her own very French holiday gift solution: "I give berets, hats, and knit scarves for every woman in the family at any age," she says. Although this might not sound very original, hats are clever gifts, especially if you get creative and buy wintry hats that are verging on silly. Wooly hats for the cold weather can be crazy, furry, and generally over the top, and you'll have as much fun buying them as your family and friends will have wearing them.

Jeff Mashie, Chaiken's creative director sticks to unsized items. "They're best," he says. "Capes, wraps, gloves, or cardigans." Nicole Miller adds, "Cashmere makes everyone happy!"

More one-note solutions here? I think so!

As for what *not* to buy, well, be careful not to choose anything you would buy directly and personally for yourself or it might look like you are not thinking of the person in mind.

Last, designer Luca Orlandi has the "family fashion dilemma" all worked out. "Get Mom new lingerie, get Dad leather pants, and your sister? Don't waste your time. She will never wear anything that you give her!"

Timeless and original fashion gifts don't always need to be things to wear, they can also be fashionable accessories or fashion-related items:

For her

✳ *A sweater.* *The* most popular of all fashion gifts, these are timeless. Knits are the easiest unsized item to buy, which makes picking something that is a good fit for your chosen recipient less stressful. You are less likely to oversize.

✳ *A wristlet bag from a luxury label.* A genius way to give a high-octane designer gift without breaking the bank.

✳ *A book on fashion.* Like this one!—Or buy an historical biography of a designer or other influential fashionista.

✳ *A magazine subscription.* It's a personalized fashion gift that keeps on giving. Try *Vogue, W, Elle, In Style,* or other fashion magazine that will appeal to the specific person. Each month when the magazine arrives in the mailbox and each time the recipient sees it, there is a reminder of the thoughtful person who gave it to her.

✳ *A membership to Bag Borrow or Steal* (a service that rents designer accessories from $5 a month). Check out www.bagborroworsteal.com.

✳ *A set of padded and or scented coat hangers.* It's a gift for the closet! Perfect for hanging new lingerie on.

✳ *A sexy boudoir-style eye mask.* Technically, this is something to wear to bed, but one made of luxury silk will definitely make bedtime look and feel more fashionable. It's also a perfect unsized item.

✳ *Silk pajamas.* Another luxury indulgence that is not hard to buy the correct size in. These are likely to be lounged around in, doing double duty as luxury loungewear.

✳ *A pretty jewelry wrap.* A jewelry wrap is a fashiony gift for someone who you think has almost everything. She can always own more than one of these, and it's a thoughtful and feminine gift for someone who travels and loves her jewels!

* *Scented bags for the underwear drawer.* Who needs moth balls anymore? Luxury herb sachets or natural-scent bags are a great behind-the-scenes fashion accessory, since they scent the clothes and keep things fresh.

* *Hollywood tape.* This inexpensive, completely invaluable, and original multiuse gift is the perfect stocking stuffer for the woman who has everything!

* *Nonslip yoga socks.* Innovative, unusual, and useful.

* *A fashion-linked charitable gift.* Make a donation to the charity of your choice or a cause that you know is close to the heart of your gift recipient by purchasing an item produced especially for this purpose! Check out the MAC Viva Glam campaign for Aids research at www.macaidsfund.org, or go to www.gapinc.com/red for fashionable purchases that fund Aids help in Africa. Or peruse the Estée Lauder sponsored PINK products that support breast cancer research at www.bcrfcure .org/part_pinkbuys_06_fashion.html. Check out Saks Fifth Avenue too. As in the past, Designer Diane von Furstenberg has produced a sellout tee to benefit women's cancer research.

* *Shoes.* Pretty shoes, designer shoes if you can afford them. Obviously, this gift is much more size specific, so purchase only with the knowledge that they may be exchanged. Shoes are one of the happiest gifts for a girl to receive, anywhere in the world. Even if they don't fit perfectly, the gesture is worth a million bucks.

For him

✳ *Tie case.* For the guy who loves his lovely ties, a tie case is great so they may be protected and travel safely with him.

✳ *Fancy shoe trees.* Same reason as the tie case but for his shoes.

✳ *Leather slippers.* Less cutesy and much more masculine and durable than any sheepskin ones. Good call!

✳ *Designer belts.* These items are really long-life holiday gifts. They can be worn casually with jeans or formally with a suit. Another plus is that it's not entirely size specific: you only need to know roughly the waist size of the person for whom you're buying.

✳ *A custom-made shirt.* A very special gift for a man who loves the way he looks. Only a truly stylish man will appreciate it. You only need a rough estimate of the waist.

✳ *New golf shirt, gloves, or socks.* He may be fanatical about the sport, but he should look like a winner too.

✳ *A waxed hunting jacket.* An outerwear jacket that is wired or customized for cell phones, iPod wires, and other devices is the perfect gift for a man who takes techno gadgets and his personal style equally seriously.

✳ *A performance-wear shirt.* Is he a cyclist? Or a skier? Pick something high tech that marries form and function. It will do its job and look spectacular at the same time.

For kids

✳ *Themed pajamas.* The easiest and often welcomed gift for boys and girls are themed pajamas. Kids always need spare pairs and the exact sizing is not so critical. Indulge their fantasy for being Batman or Cinderella, at least at bedtime.

* *A fun dress-up outfit.* Add something to his or her dress-up collection such as Cinderella or Pocahontas for her and Batman or Spiderman for him.

* *Snazzy sneakers with wheels.* The safer and more fashion-oriented option to a skateboard is well received by most kids! Being part rollerblade-part sneaker means these are a great dual-functioning addition to the wardrobe.

* *Shoes for girls.* All girls want to look like a princess and like to have a collection of "special" shoes. Expanding her Princess collection with shoes is a sure bet.

* *Sports memorabilia.* Pick something from a child's favorite sports team and you will have a winner for a gift. Football shirts, baseball caps, and tees with sports stars' names are suitable and are no-brainer gifts.

For teens

* *Trendy boots.* Be they Uggs, Frye, Converse, baseball, or other fashion boots, teens—both male and female— love new winter footwear.

* *A book on sewing.* For that budding do-it-yourself whiz who will end up designing for a big fashion house one day (or at least keep her busy modifying vintage clothes from the thrift store on Saturday afternoons).

* *A cashmere-covered hot water bottle.* Teens love cuddly stuff, and although this doesn't technically rank as a "fashion" item, the many different textiles and covers

that are obtainable make this something that can be customized to their taste.

✳ *A stylish iPod case.* Much like a jacket or sweater, the style and appearance of an iPod case is very much on the minds of teens. Purchasing a case that reflects an individual's style and coordinates with his or her wardrobe is a fashion-sensitive gift and will be much appreciated.

✳ *Bag or backpack charms.* Often inexpensive and fun, and they can never have too many.

✳ *Customized DIY fashion-tee kit.* Get an inexpensive craft kit with sparkly gems, sequins, and other embellishments, a glue gun, and some plain white tees. This is hours and hours of creative fun!

For baby

✳ *A trendy diaper bag.* Well this one is really for Mom—but a gorgeous diaper bag that Mom wears and thus wants to coordinate with her style can be a wonderful gift. Even if a mom-to-be or new mom has one, it can be great to have an alternative, and you can fill it as a baby F.E.K. with staples of baby supplies.

✳ *A baby sling.* The ultimate fashion accessory for the budding baby fashionista!

✳ *Socks or soft booties.* Infants lose these all the time, they can never have too many.

✳ *Personalized burping cloths.* Mom will be thrilled. Less of a rag (since it's worn on Mom's shoulder) and more a holiday party accessory.

✳ *Stroller wear.* Outdoor clothes or a sleep sack for baby, all coordinated. Check out such innovative websites as www.tuttibella.com; www.jenklairkids.com; www. twinkleteas.com; and www.totsonthego.com and look for handcrafted items as well as local boutiques.

WHAT TO SHOP IN DECEMBER

* Holiday gifts
* Resort items
* Snow boots and earmuffs
* Luxury sweats and totes

So it's the end of the year, you've barely got a dime to spare, and you have to stretch what you have to buy *gifts.* Luckily, there are fabulous and sometimes ready-packaged fashion gifts around at this time. For example, JCPenney's "Tux in a Box" gift set is a genius man's gift. It's a box set with a dress shirt, studs, bow tie, and cummerbund and it's always under $50. Retailers *want* you to buy fashion finds for your friends and family, and sometimes they make it really easy. Henri Bendel in New York always has something special and innovative available in the store before the holidays. It's usually a limited-edition special something like an *adampluseve* dress in an exclusive color. Liz Claiborne Apparel, which sells in many department stores such as Macy's, Dillard's, and Belk, does a great addition to their clothes around the holidays. They attach an extra "gifting" ticket to the items before they hit the racks because they know everyone is looking for gift ideas. This tag dresses up the item so that you can visualize it as a gift and gives you the option to write a short "To and From" message. There are a gazillion other ideas like this one in the stores, and that's when it pays to browse, in person or online. You get ideas for gift shopping *by* shopping.

While you're in the crazy crowded stores, if you see a burst of color mixed in with the December winter wonderland of knits and wools, it's because the *resort items* have hit the shelves. These include swimwear, hot-weather vacation clothes, shorts, dresses, and accessories to complement them. If you are heading for winter sun, get something to update your swim and summer collections. Lucky you!

Finally, around the holidays, there are often fun and fabulous lifestyle pieces lounging luxuriously in the stores. You will know them because they scream, "I'm going to the mountains," "I'm going to the spa," or "I'm going to the beach." I'm referring to those lovely luxuries such as *snow boots, furry earmuffs, luxury sweats,* or *luxury totes.* Depending on your budget, these might be your final but fabulous indulgences for the year.

TIPS FOR A LOWER TAB

If you're a dedicated sale shopper, do go shop on December 26th and 27th, two of the biggest sale days of the year. However, if like me you *are not,* it's a perfect moment to save money. Here's how: If you clean out your closet in the post-holiday hush and bring all your unworn and unwanted stuff to Goodwill, you can get a tax deduction before the end of the year. It's the perfect time and a good project that'll leave you feeling ready to face the New Year. You'll be so busy with this that you won't possibly be able to sink into any holiday blues. And it'll save you some cash—cash that you can use to restock your closet year-round!

TAKE ONE LAST LOOK

So, as the year closes and the annual fashion cycle comes full circle, how are you feeling, fashion-wise? Better equipped? More likely to grab and go in the right outfit? Better at saving money and sharper at snapping up your core items ahead of the season? And how's your wallet and bank balance? Hopefully, they're healthy too. You've probably done a great job on taking stock of your closet, and you should be excited to step out into the New Year armed with all your fresh fashion knowledge. It's quite probable that you actually *knew* some of this stuff already. But I hope this book has supplied the gentle nudge you need to get you back on the right fashion track. Now you can truly do it all on your own. And you can always refer back to a specific chapter if you feel unsure at any point. But just to give you a final checklist, see the proceeding list of essential habits for streamlining your month-by-month shopping and style. I call them "habits" because if you do them and repeat them they'll become a part of your life and you won't ever need to think about them again.

Ten crucial style habits of happening people!

1. **Create at least one F.E.K.** You will be surprised how many times you or a friend will use *something* from it.

2. **Befriend a personal shopper or sales associate at your favorite store.** It will really make shopping easier. The relationship that you cultivate will help you secure the hottest stuff as soon as it comes in, before it ever reaches the racks, and keep you posted on possible markdowns or other special in-store promotions or news.

3. **Go for vintage.** Practice shopping at flea markets and antiques fairs for vintage finds. You will have a more eclectic selection of items to get dressed up in.

4. **Know when to shop alone.** You *can* trust your own style intuition, and it's very freeing not to be swayed by your best friend or mom who pushed you toward purchases she'd like to see you dressed in. The best way around pushy friends who badger you to shop every weekend or after work is to go with them, but don't part with your cash. Find a moment to go back and try on what you've seen again when you're alone. Most stores will honor a waiting period of a day or two for an item placed on "hold."

5. **Claim a signature accessory.** Whether you are aiming to be a trendsetter or style icon, one item or category of items (like flats or big sunglasses or horse theme) will recur for you every time you get dressed. Pinpoint what this is and play it up. It will be your keystone for style.

6. **Get a watch wardrobe.** They don't have to be luxury timepieces, but changing your watch can completely

change the tone of your outfit and inspire you to figure in other complementary accessories.

7. **Get some shoe glamour.** Indulge in a pair of knock-out-drag-out-gorgeous evening shoes. They will make you feel great when you look at them, glam when you wear them, and in love every time you take them out of their box and hold them!

8. **Organize that closet.** Having the right components in your wardrobe means you're more than halfway to winning the styling battle. If you've truly got so much stuff that you can't see the wool for the linen, crash through it in one designated weekend and crop the number of items in half. If you have a storage area and are prepared to take careful inventory, then pack it away according to season. Remember to leave out seasonless separates or they'll never see the light of day. Be ruthless and dump the rest. Donate, donate, donate!

9. **Recycle what you've got.** I can't say it enough times or enough different ways: dig it out, re-rack it, reline it, cut it, sew it, and mix it with something new or unexpected. The "I've got nothing to wear" excuse doesn't fly with me. You *have* and you *can*. Prove it to yourself. Find a new life for something old but not quite finished yet.

10. **Plan your wardrobe a season ahead.** The whole purpose of *Just Try It On!* is to serve as a reminder of what is ahead and therefore what is fresh and new in the stores. When you have a head start in knowing when to shop for what, you really have a good plan. Once your seasonal key pieces are bought, you can always add on or pick up bargain extras for more choices.